THE WORLD'S
GREATEST
UNSOLVED
CRIMES

METROPOLITAN POLICE
Appeal for Assistance

MISSING

Mrs Linda Jacqueline STURLEY,
54″ tall with shoulder length,
fair hair and aged 29,
left her home in Main Road,
Biggin Hill, Kent, between 9pm
and 17 July and Saturday

...s pregnant.
...n wearing a
...dress.

DO YOU KNO...
...E YOU SEEN H...
HAVE ANY O...

Please con...
CATFOR...
Te...

...informatio...

THE WORLD'S GREATEST UNSOLVED CRIMES

ROGER BOAR

NIGEL BLUNDELL

HAMLYN

First published in 1984
by Octopus Books Limited

This edition first published in 1991 by
The Hamlyn Publishing Group Limited
part of Reed International Books
Michelin House, 81 Fulham Road
London SW3 6RB
and Auckland, Melbourne, Singapore and Toronto

Reprinted 1984, 1985, 1987, 1991, 1992, 1993 (twice)

ISBN 0 600 57231 5

A CIP catalogue record for this book is available at the British Library

Printed in Great Britain at The Bath Press, Avon

Contents

Acknowledgements

The editors would like to acknowledge the contributions of the writers and researchers whose work made this book possible. They are: Gerry Brown, Robin Corry, Rob Robbins, Brian McConnell, David Williams, Mike Parker, Marian Davison, Jack Pleasant, Frederick Rolph, Bernard Connor, Frank Garvan, Don Farmer, George Todd, Rodney Hallworth, Mark Williams, Ted Hynds, Paul Vallely and Iain Walker.

The publishers wish to thank the following organizations for their kind permission to reproduce the pictures in this book:

Mary Evans Picture Library 26, 29, 91, 117, 153, 177; Popperfoto 188; Topham Picture Library 2 left and right, 12, 31, 34–35, 34 below, 45, 49, 60, 78, 87, 88, 108, 123, 125, 137, 141, 149, 151, 157 above and below, 167, 170, 174.

Introduction

Mayhem, murder and mystery! They are the ingredients of the most intriguing crime stories of all – the crimes that go unsolved.

In most major criminal cases, there is a neat ending. The misdeed is detected, the suspect arrested and the culprit punished. The file can then be closed.

But not always. Often the massive manhunt and the painstaking investigation lead nowhere. A thief, a cheat or a homicidal monster may go free. A cunning criminal may live to strike again. Or, even when apprehended, a villain may leave an agonizing question mark over his or her foul deed.

Such cases are the very essence of whodunnits. But this book is devoted not to fiction but to fact. It reveals the astonishing, known facts about real acts of villainy ... and it probes the fascinating, missing facts that confound the law and keep a crime in the file marked 'UNSOLVED'.

Chapter
One

Crimes
Without Call

Who was R. M. Qualtrough?

William Herbert Wallace was a drab, colourless, boring man who lived a drab, colourless, boring life. He was thrifty and hard-working, mild mannered and a little snobbish, soberly dressed and utterly, utterly respectable. His idea of a night out with the boys was his regular fortnightly visit to a local café to take part in chess tournaments. A swinging party at home with his mousy wife, Julia, usually consisted of the couple playing duets on violin and piano.

Herbert's meek and unassuming manner was greatly appreciated by his employer, a solid dependable insurance company who employed him as a collector and agent. In 15 years in their employment he had proved to be utterly trustworthy. He was diligent and he never pushed for promotion.

His admirable personal qualities and those of his shy little wife made them ideal neighbours in their neat terraced house in Wolverton Street, Anfield, Liverpool. He was never known to show outbursts of exuberance or bad temper.

In fact, the jury at his trial decided, Herbert Wallace had all the characteristics of a sadistic brutal murderer.

His wife had been battered to death so violently that her brains had spilled out on to the floor. She had died at the hands of a man who deliberately laid a meticulous trail of false clues to throw the police off his scent.

There was no real evidence to connect her husband with Julia Wallace's death. In fact he had a near-perfect alibi. But then Herbert Wallace was a man who ordered his life with pedantic attention to detail.

He was too good to be true. The jury's verdict seemed to be that Wallace was so absolutely ordinary that he had to be capable of great evil . . .

In spite of flimsy police theories which hardly stood up to defence cross-examination, in spite of a complete lack of motive on the part of the accused man, in spite of a summing-up by the trial judge who virtually begged the jury to acquit him, Wallace was found guilty of his wife's murder.

He sat impassively in the dock when the verdict was returned. It was this same lack of emotion which had led him there in the first place. 'I am not guilty. I cannot say anything else,' he whispered plaintively to the court as the judge prepared to pass sentence.

The judge, Mr Justice Robert Alderson Wright, showed more distress than the convicted man. But he had no option under law. Shaken by the jury's verdict, he donned his black cap and passed the only sentence open to him: to be hanged by the neck until dead.

And the mystery man who actually bludgeoned Julia Wallace to death heaved a deep sigh of relief. He had got away with the perfect murder.

The first sign that Herbert Wallace's humdrum life was about to be shattered came with a telephone call from a complete stranger to the City Cafe in North John Street, Liverpool, at 19.15 on Monday 19 January 1931. Herbert Wallace was due at the cafe that night to exercise his rather mundane skill as a chess player. He was taking part in a tournament aptly named 'The Second Class Championship'.

But the 52-year-old insurance agent was not there to take the telephone call. A waitress answered the phone and passed it to Samuel Beattie, Captain of the chess club, who explained that Wallace had not yet arrived. Did the caller want to phone back later?

The voice on the other end of the line asked to leave a message for Wallace. The caller identified himself as 'R. M. Qualtrough' and requested that Wallace should call on him at his home at 25 Menlove Gardens East, Mossley Hill, the following night to discuss some insurance business. Beattie wrote the message on the back of an envelope.

About the same time Herbert Wallace was setting off from his home at 29 Wolverton Street to catch a tram to the City Cafe for the chess club meeting.

The Wallaces had been married for 18 years, after a two-year engagement in their home town of Harrogate, Yorkshire. Herbert had a worthy, but lowly paid, job as political agent for the local branch of the Liberal Party. When the meagre party funds could no longer support his salary, he moved to the quiet suburb of Anfield in Liverpool.

Julia, five years younger than her husband, set about making their new home in Wolverton Street neat and tidy, just like their lives. In her earlier years she had spent some time in the genteel studies of music and painting, and a small upright piano took pride of place in the parlour of their trim terraced house. As Herbert settled in to his new job as a collector for the Prudential Insurance Company, the childless couple could afford little luxuries like the £80 which Mr Wallace had spent on a microscope.

He prided himself on being a diligent amateur scientist. He even lectured part-time in chemistry at Liverpool Technical College and often he and Julia would spend the evening in the little laboratory he had built just off his bathroom, examining slides on the microscope. At the age of 50, Herbert had even started to learn the violin and accompanied Julia on the piano.

His job paid him an annual salary of £250 and the thrifty couple lived quietly within their means. Herbert had a bank savings account of £152 and Julia had her own modest savings of £90.

The Wallaces' home

As Herbert Wallace wrote in his diary: 'We seem to have pulled well together and I think we both get as much pleasure and contentment out of life as most people.'

The only times he left Julia alone were his visits to the chess club and his lectures at the technical college. But when he stepped out that night to catch his tram to the café, there was a nagging worry in his mind. There had been a spate of burglaries in Anfield in the past few weeks and Wallace often kept large sums of his insurance company's money at home. 'Don't open the door to any strangers while I'm gone, dear,' he reminded Julia as he left.

Samuel Beattie never actually saw Wallace arrive at the City Cafe but shortly after the phone call he saw him seated, taking part in a game, and he passed on Qualtrough's message.

Wallace seemed puzzled by the telephone call. He did not know any Mr Qualtrough. The address was on the other side of the sprawling Liverpool suburbs, quite outside his normal insurance sales territory. On the way home from the club that night, he quizzed other members about the location of Menlove Gardens East. Which tram should he take to get there? How long would the journey take?

The following day Wallace set out, regular as clockwork, on his appointed rounds in Anfield, collecting a premium of a few pence here, paying out a claim of a few pounds there. He returned home punctually for lunch at 14.00, went back to work for the afternoon and finished in the evening at 18.00. While Julia prepared tea, Wallace went upstairs, washed and changed and filled his jacket pocket with insurance quotation and proposal forms.

At 18.30, their meal over, Julia Wallace answered a knock at the door. It was the milk boy, 14-year-old Alan Close. He handed Mrs Wallace a pint container of milk and she took it into the kitchen to empty the contents into her own jug, returning to the front door to give the boy the dairy's can. That was the last time she was seen alive.

About 15 minutes later Herbert Wallace left the house. He walked a few hundred yards and boarded a tram in Belmont Road for the first leg of his journey to meet the mysterious Mr Qualtrough. At 19.06, after travelling a mile and a half, he switched to a second tram in Lodge Lane. His behaviour was unusual for the normally reserved Herbert Wallace. He chatted amiably to the tram conductor Tom Phillips about his high hopes of selling a big insurance policy at his destination. At 19.15 he arrived at Penny Lane and switched to a third tram to complete his five mile journey. He asked conductor Arthur Thompson to let him off at the stop nearest Menlove Gardens East.

'Don't know it,' Thompson admitted. 'But we stop in Menlove Avenue. Just ask around, it's bound to be near there.'

For the next half hour Wallace tramped busily around the streets of Mossley Hill. He found Menlove Gardens North. He found Menlove Gardens West and Menlove Gardens South. But no Menlove Gardens East. He knocked on the door of Mrs Katie Mather at No 25 Menlove Gardens West and she told him there was no Menlove Gardens East. He remembered his Prudential Insurance supervisor, Joseph Crewe, lived nearby and found his home and knocked on the door. He got no reply.

He met Police Constable James Sargent on his beat in nearby Allerton Road and was advised to go to the local post office to check a street directory for Mr Qualtrough's address. Wallace agreed. Then he remarked on the late hour.

'Yes, almost eight o'clock', the policeman agreed. There was no directory available at the post office and Wallace found a newsagent's shop. He pestered the owner, Mrs Lily Pinches, into checking the names of customers on the shop's newspaper delivery round, explaining his errand to her in great detail. No, she confirmed, there is no Menlove Gardens East.

Wallace gave up and went home.

He arrived back at Wolverton Street shortly before 21.00 and his neighbours, John Johnston and his wife Florence, saw him struggling with the handle of his back door. Finally he managed to get the door open and went inside. The Johnstons were still watching as Wallace emerged a few moments later and calmly invited them in. 'It's Julia,' he explained flatly. 'Come and see, she has been killed.'

Within minutes the police were summoned. Julia Wallace was dead. Her skull had been battered by ten separate blows, any single one of which would have been fatal. There was blood everywhere. A total of £4 was missing from the little cash box in the kitchen cabinet. She had been killed, the forensic experts decided later, between 18.30 and 20.00 that night.

Herbert Wallace appeared to be almost unmoved by the sight of his dead wife. Later that night he left the murder house and moved in with his brother's family a few miles away. The detectives, meanwhile, moved in to 29 Wolverton Street. And the tongues wagged furiously.

Why had Herbert Wallace talked of his business so freely to tram conductors and total strangers in his quest to find Menlove Gardens East? Had he deliberately drawn the patrolling policeman's attention to the time? And who was R. M. Qualtrough, whose call the night before had lured him away from home? If the address in Mossley Hill never existed, did R. M. Qualtrough exist?

On 2 February 1931, a week after the body of Julia Wallace was buried in Anfield Cemetery, Herbert Wallace was charged with her murder. Cautioned by the police, he said simply and sadly: 'What can I say in answer to a charge of which I am absolutely innocent?' The press headlines had become so sensational and strident that when the trial opened at St George's Hall seven weeks later, even the prosecution made little objection to a defence request that no residents of the city of Liverpool should sit on the jury.

The prosecution made much of a key piece of evidence. They had traced the source of the call from 'R. M. Qualtrough'. By sheer chance, the call to the City Cafe the night before Julia Wallace's murder had to be routed through a telephone supervisor because the coin mechanism in the public phone box had been faulty. The call and the defect were duly logged. The call had come from Anfield 1627, a kiosk in Rochester Road, only 400 yards from Wallace's home.

Of course Wallace was not at the café to receive the call from 'Qualtrough', prosecuting counsel Edward Hemmerde, explained triumphantly. For the same reason, 'Qualtrough' couldn't phone back later to speak to Wallace after he arrived at the chess club, because Herbert Wallace was 'R. M. Qualtrough'.

Wallace, Hemmerde claimed, had made the telephone call himself then sprinted for a tram and arrived at the café to receive the message he had phoned through as 'Qualtrough'.

His pestering inquiries of tram conductors, the policeman and the residents of Mossley Hill the following night were all part of the plan to establish his alibi, the prosecutor insisted. And Wallace's unflurried demeanour when he returned home and found his wife's body was the action of a man who already knew murder had been committed.

Herbert Wallace's defence counsel, Roland Oliver, outlined his case simply. His client had not committed the murder and it was not for the defence to prove who had wielded the murder weapon. Wallace was not 'Qualtrough' and the defence did not need to establish the identity of the mystery man. Wallace made a fuss of finding Menlove Gardens East, he explained, because it was a break from his usual routine, a chance to earn the unexpected bonus of a sale. He was displaying an emotion that was rare for him: excitement. He had only reverted to character when he found his wife's body. He became placid and introspective. Wallace had no motive for killing his own wife.

By all the rules of criminal law, Roland Oliver was absolutely right. The police had no evidence, only suspicions. Herbert Wallace had to be presumed innocent. But on the fourth and final day of the trial, the jury took only an hour to reach their verdict: Guilty.

It is almost routine for a judge to express his agreement with a jury's verdict in a complex, tasking case. Mr Justice Wright, however, did not even offer them a word of thanks for their efforts. He pronounced the mandatory sentence of death by hanging.

The defence lodged an immediate appeal and a week after he should have been hanged Wallace was taken from the condemned cell to London, to appear at the Royal Courts of Justice in the Strand. Far from the hysteria and prejudice of Liverpool, three judges sifted through the hard evidence against Wallace. After a two-day hearing they retired for 45 minutes and pronounced their verdict: Appeal allowed, conviction quashed.

Wallace left the courtroom free – but spiritually broken.

Two days later when he returned home, Liverpool police pointedly announced they would not be re-opening their investigation into Julia Wallace's murder. The cruel implication was not lost on Wallace's hostile neighbours and his workmates. The insurance company gave him a desk job to try to shield him and a year later he retired on a pension.

In February 1933, just over two years after the death of his wife, Herbert Wallace became ill with a recurring kidney disease and died in a local hospital. Five days later he was buried in Anfield Cemetery beside his beloved Julia.

So who murdered Julia Wallace? Who was R. M. Qualtrough? There were only 14 people in the whole of Liverpool with the name Qualtrough and the police interviewed and cleared them all. In the atmosphere of outrage which followed the murder, Liverpool police reached the single-minded conclusion that Wallace was guilty. Squads of detectives armed with stop-watches and timetables spent days riding on trams and walking briskly around Anfield trying to demolish his timing of events.

Herbert Wallace had his own suspicions. In the long nights of lonely agony after his wife's murder, he wondered which of his small circle of acquaintances knew he was due at the City Cafe that fateful night and left the tantalising telephone message for him. Julia, he knew, would only have opened the door to a familiar face. Even facing the hangman's noose, shy Herbert Wallace could not bring himself to scream in righteous anger and point a forceful finger of accusation.

He apologetically mentioned the names of two men to the Liverpool detectives investigating the case. Both men were in their early twenties and both were former employees of the insurance company. At different times, they had both parted company from the insurance firm after cash shortages were found in their accounts. On separate occasions, they had filled in for Wallace on his rounds when he was ill. They knew all about his social routine, about his chess club meetings. And they knew that on some Tuesday nights, as on the night Julia was murdered, the cash box in the kitchen could hold as much as £50. Indeed when they stood in for him they had been inside his home and had handled the cash box. Julia would have readily opened the door to them, knowing they were former colleagues of her husband.

Police records show that detectives only interviewed one of these men – and even then accepted without question his assurance that he had an alibi for the night of the murder.

The police concentrated all their energies on the man they wanted ... the mousey little insurance agent whom everyone so desperately wanted to believe was a murdering monster.

Advertisement of Death

The voice on the telephone was smooth, fluent and persuasive ... and instantly Josephine Backshall was cocooned in a web of friendly familiarity. She knew the caller's voice well and had been longing for him to ring. After all, he was helping her to earn £100, a big enough sum of 'pin-money' to make a world of difference to the family budget.

There was nothing in the least shady about the job as a part-time model that Josephine was beginning to enjoy. In fact, the thought that the small advertisement she had placed in the local paper could be misconstrued in anything like an unseemly light had never crossed the mind of the house-proud, 39-year-old mother-of-three, who sang for the local church choir and was a leader of the town's Brownies troupe. And the idea that there could be anything sinister about the man who answered her advertisement and, in a 'trial session', had photographed her on the front lawn of the family's tidy, middle-class semi-detached home in Maldon, Essex, would have seemed too outrageous to contemplate.

The man, she told her husband Mike, seemed like a 'good sort'. And, as she spoke to him again on the 'phone, she realized that what he was offering her would be her biggest job so far: £100 for a day's work – probably, she thought, modelling for something no more glamorous than a cheap cosmetic firm.

The caller talked on, cool, collected, giving the impression of a very pleasant personality. A meeting was arranged for that evening and, after kissing her husband goodbye, she walked through the front door of their spruce home for the last time.

Three days later, at about 12.00 on Friday, 1 November 1974, she was found strangled to death.

Her body had been dumped in a shallow pond by the side of a lonely lovers' lane. Her hands were bound in front of her with a length of cord strapped tightly to her wrists. An identical cord was lashed to her neck.

Josephine Backshall, the church-going good neighbour who enjoyed an innocent life of simple pleasures, was killed because she put her faith in a confidence trickster. She trusted a mystery man whose identity the police have spent more than 100,000 man-hours trying to discover, with not a single clue to put them on the trail of a quarry whose disappearance has made the Josephine Backshall case one of Britain's most perplexing unsolved crimes.

No fewer than 40 detectives were assigned to the case in the first year of one of the biggest, yet most baffling, investigations of its kind. More than 19,000 members of the public were interviewed. All of them had either the Christian name of Pete or Dave, or the surname of Thomson or Johnson. It was a combination of those names that fitted the clues that Josephine had given her family and friends. It was to them that she had spoken of the man with the camera who was setting her up not, as she believed as a part-time model, but as a victim of brutal murder, even the motive for which has never been established.

Thousands of car registration plates were later painstakingly checked and rechecked by police trying to find the killer's car – possibly a blue Ford which was seen pulling away from the Fountain public house in Good Easter, Essex, on the night Josephine kept her fateful rendezvous with her killer.

Detectives established that Josephine and the man she so easily trusted did stop for a drink – one half-pint of beer each – at the Fountain about an hour after she had left her home. He was presumed to have picked her up nearby and taken her there after a 'business dinner' at a Chinese restaurant – an assumption based on the fact that forensic experts discovered the remains of Chinese food in her stomach.

Publican's wife Joan Jones became the last witness to the rendezvous of a killer and his victim when she saw the couple in the Fountain's saloon bar. 'I caught only a fleeting glance of him,' she says. 'He was a tall man. His head touched a line of beer mugs hanging over the bar. He never actually seemed to face me and, on reflection, it seemed almost as though he was trying to not let anyone get too close a look at him'.

Mrs Jones identified Josephine from a cine film containing family holiday shots which detectives showed her. 'I remembered her at once,' she says. 'She was an attractive woman. She had sat in the corner of the bar with the man and had seemed totally at her ease.'

For months, police kept details of the Fountain meeting secret in the hope that the killer would retrace his steps. It was a forlorn hope.

The only other potential lead detectives had to go on was a 'French connection'. A keen-eyed policewoman found a cosmetics sample in Josephine's bedroom which was one of a very limited batch which had been imported from France prior to a sales drive. Could the killer, detectives pondered, have been using Josephine to model this new range?

Inquiries again, however, came to nought – as did a scrupulous check on every photographic studio in both England and France from which a killer might have been tempted by Josephine's original advertisement, which read:

'Lady, late 30s, seeks part-time employment. Own transport. Anything considered. Previous experience: banking. Able to type.' Underneath was her home telephone number.

Josephine Backshall

It was the sort of advertisement often used to skirt the law as a method of offering sex-for-sale. A senior officer on the case later described it as 'positively naive'. He added:

> 'We all know what the phrase "anything considered" is taken to mean. The great irony and tragedy of this case is that any innuendo couldn't have been further from the truth. Mrs Backshall was a God-fearing woman – and that sort of interpretation of her advert simply wouldn't have occurred to her. It seems more than likely that her own innocence – a rare attribute in this day and age – may have, tragically, led her to set herself up as a victim of murder.'

Other senior officers have described the Josephine Backshall case as the 'most frustrating' they have ever worked on. But, as far as has been possible, they have managed to piece together this diary of death:

A few days after Josephine placed her ad, a male caller telephoned to offer her work 'modelling for cosmetics'. An appointment was made for a week later, 15 miles from Josephine's home, at Witham, Essex. The man never showed up. He 'phoned the following day, rearranged the appointment, and again failed to appear. Two weeks later, the 'phone rang once more – and Josephine happily arranged yet another meeting.

This time, the couple did meet. The 'photographer' took a series of pictures of Josephine on the front lawn of her home during the day. By that stage, Josephine's husband had begun to believe her part-time job would come to nothing and, ironically, expressed mild doubt as to the authenticity of the cameraman who was promising his wife tidy sums for what seemed simple work. Josephine allayed those fears, saying that the man seemed perfectly genuine and, indeed, a 'good sort'.

The telephone rang again on Tuesday, 29 October 1974 and the last, fateful meeting was arranged. Josephine left the family home in Norfolk Close, Maldon at about 18.00, driving to Witham in her red Ford Cortina, registration number BVW 374L.

Detectives have established that she was seen at Witham's Colingwood Road car park between 18.30 and 19.00. A passer-by told them her car may have broken down, because he saw her looking into the engine with the bonnet raised close to the car park entrance. Some time before 19.00, however, she must have met her killer.

There is a time gap between then and three days later, when a telephone line worker made the gruesome discovery of her body in the ditch at Bury Green on the Essex and Hertfordshire border.

The killer had left no clue behind. Chief Superintendent Jack Moulder, who still keeps the Josephine Backshall case file open, can only say: 'Someone, somewhere must know him.'

The Green Bicycle Murder

The tragic death of pretty Bella Wright would have been written off as a fatal road accident if it had not been for the shrewd curiosity of a young country constable.

For when 21-year-old Bella was found dead on a quiet road near the village of Stretton in Leicestershire, with her bicycle lying on the grass verge, it added a terrible weight to the complaints of the locals who cursed the reckless and speeding drivers in their peaceful little communities.

The dead girl's face was deeply gouged and matted with blood. Gravel from the roadway was embedded in her face where she had pitched forward from her bicycle and struck the ground. She had obviously been run off the road by some ruthless motorist, the villagers insisted. It was July 1919 and clattering motor cars were not yet a commonplace sight in the quiet countryside. Their drivers, according to popular rural opinion, terrified the farm animals and were a mortal danger to peaceful cyclists and rambling pedestrians.

A cursory examination of Bella's body by a local doctor seemed to confirm that opinion. He concluded that something had caused Bella to lose control of her bicycle, throwing her into the road where she died of loss of blood and head injuries.

The local constable, however, had some nagging doubts. He went to search the scene of the road accident for any further clues to showing exactly how Bella had met her death.

As he poked around the grass verges on either side of the narrow road, the constable found the blood-spattered body of a dead carrion crow. But there were no tyre marks near the bird. He turned its body over with the tip of his boot and continued his search. A few feet away, where Bella's bicycle had lain, he found another object which caught his attention. It was a spent bullet, pushed down into the soft earth by the imprint of a horse's hoof.

A fresh examination of Bella's body showed the grim truth about her death. In the swollen blood-stained tissue below her left eye was a bullet hole. Hidden in the tangled mass of her hair was an exit wound. Bella had been shot clean through the head.

The police search switched from the pursuit of a hit and run driver to the hunt for a cold-blooded murderer.

The night before Bella died she had been on one of her frequent cycling jaunts, riding to the village postbox to send a letter to her sweetheart, a young sailor aboard a warship which was stationed 240 km (150 miles) away in Portsmouth. The pretty brunette who lived with her parents had made male admirers, but she only flirted with them. Her deepest affections were reserved for the sailor she hoped would soon ask her to marry him.

Bella had finished a long tiring night shift as a mill hand in a factory in nearby Leicester when she returned home on Saturday 5 July and slept until late afternoon.

After a quick meal when she woke she cycled off briskly to post her letter, telling her parents she might pay a visit to her uncle, a roadworker, who lived not very far away.

When Bella arrived at her uncle's cottage two hours later, she was not alone. As she went inside the cottage a sallow-faced man waited outside for her, seated astride his green bicycle.

Bella's uncle, George Measures, teased her about her strange companion. She smiled: 'Oh him, I don't really know him at all. He has been riding alongside me for a few miles but he isn't bothering me at all. He's just chatting about the weather.'

When Bella was ready to leave for home an hour later, her uncle glanced through the window and saw the man with the green bicycule was still waiting outside. 'Oh, I do hope he doesn't get boring,' Bella laughed coyly. 'I'll soon cycle fast enough to give him the slip.'

The man with the green bicycle grinned happily at Bella when she left the cottage and pedalled his bicycle to join her as they rode off together in the warm summer evening's air.

An hour later a farmer driving his cattle along the peaceful Burton-Overy road, found Bella's body. An inquest on the dead girl returned a verdict of 'murder by person or persons unknown'. The vital witness, the man with the green bicycle could not be traced.

But his bicycle was found, seven months later, when a barge skipper on a canal outside Leicester found that a line trailing from his boat had snagged on a piece of junk on the canal bed. The junk brought to the surface was the frame of a green bicycle. Policemen who probed the muddy canal bottom soon uncovered a gun holster and a dozen revolver cartridges.

One of the serial numbers on the bicycle frame had been hastily filed off. But another identifying number inside the saddle support led police to the local dealer for the bicycle maker and then to the identity of the man who had bought it ten years before.

The owner of the bicycle was railway draughtsman Ronald Light, a moody shell-shocked veteran of World War 1 with a fascination for guns. He had been invalided out of the Army and had lived in Leicester until six months after Bella's murder.

When police traced 34-year-old Light he had left his home in Leicester he shared with his widowed mother and taken a job about 100 km (60 miles away) as a school teacher in Cheltenham. He was arrested and brought back to Leicester to be charged with the murder of Bella Wright.

His trial began at Leicester Assizes in June 1920 and from the opening speech of the prosecution the circumstantial evidence was stacked mercilessly against Ronald Light. Witness after witness identified him as the man with the green bicycle and a young maidservant from Light's own home told how he kept firearms and ammunition in the attic.

The prosecution amply proved that Ronald Light had been the mystery man who cycled off with Bella just before her death. Light himself admitted filing the serial number off his bicycle and throwing it, with the holster and cartridges, into the canal a few weeks after the murder.

The only arguably weak point in the prosecution's case was the lack of motive. Bella had not been sexually assaulted or robbed. Even though Light denied killing her, claiming that they parted company at the village crossroads, the irrefutable testimony seemed certain to lead him to the gallows.

One other piece of evidence seemed to cloud the case, almost irrelevantly. The bullet found by the village constable had several marks on it. The marks were caused by it passing through the dead girl's skull and the crushing effect of the steel-shod horse's hoof which had ground it into the earth. There was even one mark which might have been caused by a ricochet.

When Ronald Light gave evidence in his own defence, he seemed at first to be damning himself. He admitted trailing around after Bella on his bicycle on the night of her death, pestering her for the use of a spanner and a pump because his own cycle had developed a loose wheel and a flat tyre.

He told the jury of his own sad and tortured mental history: how he cracked up after three years of savage war in the frontline trenches, and how he was classified as a shell-shock victim and sent back to England in the closing stages of the war for psychiatric treatment.

But the effect of his testimony on the jury was electric. In a firm clear voice, without a trace of hesitation or emotion, Light told the court: 'I was an artillery gunner in the trenches from 1915 to 1918 when I was sent home a broken man. I kept my holster and ammunition because they were wrapped in a bag attached to my stretcher when they took me from the front. The Army kept my service revolver.

'When Bella Wright was murdered I knew from newspaper reports the next day that she was the girl I had been with just before she died. I knew the police wanted to question me.'

Staring blankly and coldly into space, Light admitted: 'I became a coward again. I never told a living soul what I knew. I got rid of everything which could have connected me with her. I was afraid.'

The jury looked at the gaunt face of the anguished war veteran before they retired to consider their verdict. They returned three hours later and pronounced him 'not guilty'.

As Light walked from the court a free man, the sharp-eyed constable who had turned her death into a murder investigation, blamed himself for one flaw in his inspired detective work...

The body of the dead carrion crow in the field. He had kicked it aside with hardly a second glance.

Had the bloodied crow also been blasted by a bullet from the same gun which killed Bella Wright? Had the same bullet ripped through the crow in flight and found a second, innocent human target? Could the bullet have ricochetted from a tree and ended Bella's young life?

Without the evidence of the crow and perhaps of further bullets and footprints at the scene, no one would ever know. But it was not beyond the bounds of possibility that an amateur marksman had been taking potshots at the sinister black shapes of the carrion crows in the field beside the country road.

Was there somewhere a thoughtless gunman who knew his wild shooting had killed an unsuspecting girl and who had fled from the scene to keep his terrified secret? A gunman infinitely more cowardly than the shell-shocked, broken ex-soldier Ronald Light.

The Enigma of Nuremberg

The teenage boy who appeared from nowhere, staggering through the streets of Nuremberg, Germany, on Whit Monday 1828, acted as if he was injured or drunk.

He walked unsteadily up to a complete stranger, a local cobbler, and gave him a letter addressed to the Captain of the 6th Cavalry Regiment, then stationed in the city, and mumbled repeatedly: 'I want to be a soldier like my father was.'

The cobbler helped the boy to walk with difficulty to the police station where the lad waited until the cavalry officer was summoned. At the police station the letter was opened and the senior police officer and the cavalryman read the poignant and bitter message.

The letter explained: 'I send you a boy who is anxious to serve his king in the Army. He was left at my house on 7 October 1812, and I am only a poor labourer. I have ten children of my own to bring up. I have not let him outside since 1812.'

With cruel indifference, the letter added: 'If you do not want to keep him, kill him or hang him up a chimney.'

The letter was unsigned and the police and the army officer sadly assumed that the 16-year-old boy, abandoned as a baby, was still unwanted. The scrawled message seemed to explain his peculiar behaviour, unable to walk properly on feet as soft as a baby's and with an infant vocabulary of only a few words. But the lad could write his own name in a firm, legible hand – Caspar Hauser.

The jailer in Nuremberg was fascinated by the boy and kept him in a room in his own quarters where he could watch him through a secret opening. It took him only a few days of careful observation before he decided that Caspar was neither a born idiot nor a young madman. With loving patience, the jailer, using sign language, taught Caspar to talk, noting how quickly and eagerly the boy began to learn new skills.

Within six weeks the burgomaster of Nuremberg had been summoned to the jail to hear the first halting details from Caspar of his wretched life.

All Caspar could remember was being kept in a small cell, about 1.8 m (6 ft) long, 1.2 m (4 ft) wide and 1.5 m (5 ft) high. The shutters on the window of the cell were kept permanently closed and he slept in threadbare clothes on a bed of straw. He saw nobody and heard virtually nothing all the years he was there, living on a diet of bread and water he found in the cell when he awoke each day. Sometimes, he revealed, the water tasted bitter and made him fall asleep. Every time this happened, he woke up to find his hair had been cut and his nails trimmed.

After years of isolation, Caspar recalled, a hand reached into his cell from behind and gave him a sheet of paper and a pen. The hand guided him each day until he could write his name and repeat the phrase: 'I want to be a soldier ...'

One morning his cell was unlocked and he was taken out into the street, into daylight and the company of other people for the first time in his life. It was the first time, too, that he wore shoes.

In the confusion of unfamiliar sights and sounds, Caspar remembered nothing until he found himself in Nuremberg with the letter in his hand.

The boy's story touched the burgomaster and the people of Nuremberg and soon young Caspar was 'adopted' by a Professor Daumer who began the task of educating the teenager into the ways of the world around him.

In a few months Caspar was transformed from a stumbling retarded child to a bright intelligent young man. With his mysterious background creating a

Caspar Hauser

buzz of excitement in his new home town, he became a much sought after guest in the homes of curious philosophers and wealthy intellectuals. And Nuremberg society soon began to remark on Caspar's startling physical resemblance to the members of the families of the grand dukes of Baden, the rulers of the province. Rumours abounded, the most popular being that Caspar was of noble birth and that his childhood isolation had been heartlessly planned to prevent him succeeding to power as a Baden prince.

At the time of Caspar's birth, two of the princes of the Baden family in direct line of succession had died in mysterious circumstances. The people of Nuremberg were convinced that Caspar Hauser was an unwanted son of the royal family, born to the Grand Duke Karl and his wife the Grand Duchess Stephanie.

Grand Duchess Stephanie had indeed given birth to a child sixteen years earlier, but she never saw the baby. Scheming palace doctors had told her that her baby had died soon after birth of cerebral meningitis, a diagnosis confirmed by a post-mortem examination.

And when Grand Duke Karl became seriously ill in 1829, he had no son and heir to succeed him.

Caspar, by that time, had been in Nuremberg for a year, living with Professor Daumer and growing in reputation as a personable, intelligent young man of distinct ability and culture.

As the Grand Duke's health failed, in October 1829, Caspar's already bitterly unhappy young life was almost ended. He was attacked and stabbed by a masked assailant in the basement of Professor Daumer's house, but he survived his wounds.

The following year the Grand Duke died and the royal succession passed to another line of the family, the sons of the Countess of Hochberg.

A few months later an eccentric English nobleman, said by many to be a friend of the Hochberg family, appeared in Nuremberg to petition the courts to become Caspar's guardian in place of Professor Daumer. Philip, the 4th Earl of Stanhope, won his court plea in spite of local opposition. And so, out of public sight, another period of isolation began for the wretched Caspar. He was taken away from his new found friends in Nuremberg on Lord Stanhope's orders and lodged with a surly Protestant pastor in the town of Ansbach, 20 miles away.

With Caspar safely out of the way, Lord Stanhope lost interest in his new foster son, leaving him to his miserable existence with Pastor Meyer.

On 11 December 1833 Caspar, then 21 years old and working as an apprentice bookbinder, was returning to his dismal lodgings through a park when he was stopped by a stranger. The man asked his name and when Caspar replied, he stabbed him repeatedly. Badly wounded, Caspar staggered back to Pastor Meyer's home. But the preacher never informed the police, cruelly taunting Caspar that he had inflicted the wounds himself to get attention. Three days later Caspar Hauser died in agony.

Hearing of his death, the Grand Duchess Stephanie was reported to have broken down and wept, sobbing that she believed the young man had really been the son she was told had died in infancy.

But none of his friends or the German courts could ever prove the background of the boy with no history and no future. They could never solve the riddle of who had locked him away for the first 16 years of his hopeless life, or who the mysterious assassins were who finally succeeded in killing him.

The boy who came from nowhere was buried in the churchyard at Ansbach. On his tombstone was the simple epitaph: 'Here lies Caspar Hauser, enigma.'

Sherlock Holmes' Real Case

It was a murder case worthy of the cold, calculating detective powers of Sherlock Holmes. An elderly widow had been battered to death by a brutal murderer who had rifled through her files of personal papers and who had, inexplicably, stolen just one cheap brooch from her valuable collection of diamonds and other gems.

A tall, dark-haired man of about 30 had been seen by witnesses walking calmly away from the murder house in Glasgow. It had not taken long for Scottish policemen, acting under the pressure of public outrage, to arrest a suspect who was tried for the murder and sentenced to hang.

Twenty-four hours before the convicted man, gems dealer Oscar Slater, was due to meet the executioner, his sentence was commuted to life imprisonment. Although his life was spared, he still faced a grim existence of hard labour in prison until his dying day. Yet there were some lingering doubts about the case ... fears that Oscar Slater was no more than an innocent scapegoat.

But who could prove his innocence? Who could sift through the evidence with enough authority and thoroughness to overturn the verdict of a powerful

Sir Arthur Conan Doyle

court backed by the full might of the Scottish legal system? Sherlock Holmes, that's who – in the form of the creator of the fictional detective, author Sir Arthur Conan Doyle.

Conan Doyle was disturbed by the case of Oscar Slater when he read of the murder investigation and conviction in the scholarly legal work *Notable Scottish Trials*. The book outlined how, on little more than suspicion and circumstantial evidence, Slater had been found guilty of murdering 82-year-old Miss Marion Gilchrist at her home in Queen's Terrace, West Princes Street, Glasgow, on 21 December 1908.

Miss Gilchrist had lived the life of a virtual recluse in her home, attended only by a young maidservant, 21-year-old Helen Lambie, and seeing only rare visitors, mainly relatives. The spinster's only pleasure in life seemed to come from the loving care of her collection of diamonds, valued at £3,000.

On the night her mistress died, Helen Lambie had followed her usual practice of leaving the house around 19.00 to buy the evening newspaper. Miss Gilchrist remained inside, secure behind the double-locked doors of her home. The outer door, leading to the street, was held only by a latch which could be opened by a cord from inside the apartment if Miss Gilchrist recognized a visitor at the street door.

A few minutes after Helen left, downstairs neighbour Arthur Adams heard the noise of a heavy fall from the apartment above and went to investigate. The outer door was open but the double-locked apartment door was still secure. As he stood there puzzled, Helen returned with the evening paper and the couple unlocked the door and went in. Just as they entered the apartment, a tall, well-dressed man walked calmly past them and into the street. Inside, Marion Gilchrist was dead in the dining-room, her skull crushed.

While Adams went to raise the alarm, Helen Lambie ran the short distance to the home of Marion Gilchrist's niece, Mrs Margaret Birrell, and told her she had recognized the man who had walked from the apartment. But the niece, in a burst of outrage, told Helen Lambie she must be mistaken and she must not 'smear the man's reputation' in any statement to the police.

The police took only five days to produce some results to still the public outcry which followed the murder. They learned that gem dealer Oscar Slater, who lived not far from the murdered woman, had pawned a brooch of about the same value as the missing one. They also discovered that he and his young French mistress had fled from Scotland aboard the liner *Lusitania* using assumed names.

Police pursued the couple to New York where Slater was arrested and, protesting his innocence, agreed to waive extradition formalities and return to Glasgow.

Oscar Slater's trial

At his trial the witnesses, with some hesitation, identified him as the mystery man. Slater, a German Jew, claimed: 'I know nothing about this affair, absolutely nothing.' But the jury found him guilty by a majority verdict. Slater suffered three weeks in the condemned cell before his reprieve.

The few doubts about Slater's innocence were carefully noted in the book which Conan Doyle read and it was enough to arouse his interest. He began to examine the case with the same fresh uncluttered mind that he had devoted to his fictional super-sleuth, Sherlock Holmes of Baker Street.

Three years after the trial, after careful study of the transcripts of the court proceedings and correspondence with witnesses, Conan Doyle caused an uproar with his book, *The Case of Oscar Slater*. In the same calm style as Holmes, he punched gaping holes in the prosecution case.

The brooch which had first drawn suspicion on Slater had been pawned three weeks before the murder. Slater, Conan Doyle pointed out, had fled with his mistress under assumed names because he wanted to give the slip to his domineering, grasping wife. Slater's own lifestyle, as a gambler and womanizer, had probably prejudiced the puritanical Scottish jury against him.

Conan Doyle demolished the conflicting evidence of witnesses, some of whom claimed that the mystery murderer had been clean-shaven, others who said he was bearded. And, drawing on his own forensic expertise, he pointed out that when Slater's entire wardrobe of clothes was seized in his luggage aboard the *Lusitania*, not a single trace of blood was found on any of them.

The 'Sherlock Holmes' investigation produced immediate demands for a re-trial or public inquiry. But the wheels of justice grind slowly. It took 18 years before Oscar Slater was released by the newly appointed Scottish Court of Criminal Appeal on the technicality that the judge at his trial had misdirected the jury. Slater was awarded £6,000 in compensation.

But Arthur Conan Doyle never published the final chapter of his important murder investigation. 'Sherlock Holmes' had proved Slater's innocence. But had he ever uncovered the real identity of the killer of Marion Gilchrist?

Shortly before he died in 1930, Conan Doyle revealed to a friend:

'I knew I had a difficult enough job in getting Oscar Slater freed. That was the most important objective I had to achieve. If I had tried at the same to lay the blame for the murder on the real guilty man, it might have prejudiced Slater's chances of release.

But I believe I know the identity of the real murderer, a man who was protected by the police because he was a prominent citizen who desperately wanted something from the private papers of Marion Gilchrist. He has gone unpunished. But it is more important to me that an innocent man is free. I am satisfied.'

Dead Men Cannot Talk

The liner *Georges Phillipar* was one of the best designed cruise ships afloat when she was launched by her French builders from the slipway at St Nazaire in 1930.

It took almost two years to fit out the 17,300 tonne (17,000 ton) ship to carry up to 1,000 passengers in sumptuous luxury in richly panelled cabins with comfortable, efficient air conditioning. And no expense was spared to guarantee their safety, with an automatic sprinkler system and the latest fire-fighting appliances.

Yet the fire which broke out on D Deck on the liner's maiden voyage, a round trip to China, spread with devastating speed, killing 53 passengers and sending the pride of the French liner fleet to the bottom of the Red Sea.

The commission of inquiry in Paris which later investigated the sinking of the *Georges Phillipar* could find no firm evidence that faulty electrical design had caused the blaze, or that the fire had been accidental. They left only a tantalizing, inconclusive hint ... that powerful international assassins had turned the liner into a floating fire-bomb just to kill one VIP passenger, a crusading French journalist.

Freelance writer Albert Londres had joined the *Georges Phillipar* in April 1932 in Shanghai for the return leg of its maiden voyage. He had spent almost a year in Indo-China on a gruelling and dangerous assignment and his carefully guarded notebook was crammed with information which would have caused public outrage against the profiteering industrialists of London, Paris and Berlin..

Millions of readers throughout Europe were waiting and wondering what scandalous subject the best-selling author would choose for his next devastating report. In his first book, *The Road to Buenos Aires*, published only three years before, he had exposed the vile white slave trade of young women from the brothels of Marseilles and Hamburg to South America. It earned him the undying hatred of the French and German vice kings.

Undeterred, Londres went on to expose a similar traffic in young European girls to the houses of pleasure in Shanghai, and followed this up with an investigation of the terrorist group who had assassinated the King of Yugoslavia on French soil.

Now he had completed his damning examination of the deadly arms trade in the Far East, where the Japanese Imperial armies were gearing themselves for an expansive war of aggression and the bandit Chinese war lords were slaughtering their own countrymen in their bloody battles to gain control of vast areas of China and Manchuria.

Word quickly spread among enthusiastic European publishers that Albert Londres was on his way home with a manuscript that would light a fuse underneath the European millionaire arms suppliers, the Merchants of Death.

Londres was safely installed in his cabin, working on the notes for his new book when the liner docked briefly at Saigon, the capital of French Indo-China, and took aboard more travellers, mainly French colonial officials and their families. With a complement of 800 passengers, the liner called at Singapore, Penang and Ceylon, en route for the Red Sea, the Suez Canal and the French Mediterranean port of Marseilles.

On the night of 15 May as Londres worked alone in his cabin, the other passengers gathered on deck for a dinner dance in the sultry evening air, admiring the twinkling lights of the Arabian coast and waving to the crew of the Russian tanker *Sovietskya Neft* which passed less than a mile astern.

Around midnight the master of the *Georges Phillipar*, Captain Anton Vicq,

Above: The liner *Georges Phillipar* on her maiden voyage,
a round trip to China. No expense had been spared in the design of this
luxurious ship.
Left: The *Georges Phillipar*, almost burnt out by the
mysterious fire in which 53 passengers died.

retired to his cabin, bidding goodnight to the last of the dinner-dance revellers who stayed on the starlit deck, sipping chilled champagne.

Two hours later he was roused by the officer of the watch who warned him that a passenger cabin on D Deck was ablaze. When he made an examination in portside Number 5 cabin, Captain Vicq noted that 'It was not a local accident, but a fire appearing to become general and widespread.'

As he retreated along the deck corridor to the sound of the alarm, Captain Vicq was confronted by Nurse Yvonne Valentin who screamed that her cabin, Number 7, was also engulfed in flames. Between the two, in cabin Number 6 on D deck, writer Albert Londres was unaware of the drama.

Trying vainly to contain the blaze, Captain Vicq ordered all portholes to be closed and stopped the liner's engines. Within minutes the flames had spread to the bridge and the captain gave the order to abandon ship.

As the lifeboats were lowered the radio operator broadcast a frantic series of sos messages. But his transmission was cut suddenly short when his radio failed and power from the generator ceased. Following his well rehearsed emergency procedure, the radio operator reached for the sealed locker which held an ample supply of spare batteries – the batteries were missing.

As passengers wrapped wet towels round their faces to fight their way through the blinding acrid smoke, Captain Vicq and his crew calmly organized the evacuation of the ship. All floating furniture which could be used as liferafts was heaved overboard and terrified passengers were helped over the stern of the liner into the warm still waters of the sea.

The brief burst of pleading on the ship's radio had been enough to summon a rescue flotilla to its aid, including the Soviet tanker, two British steamers, a Japanese cargo ship and two other ocean liners.

The task of saving the souls in the lifeboats and clinging to the rafts was carried out speedily and most of them were soon aboard the mercy vessels. The stricken liner burned for three days in a column of flame which could be seen for 60 km (40 miles). When the *Georges Phillipar* finally heeled over, she sank within two minutes.

But no trace was ever found of the body of Albert Londres who had been trapped in his cabin between the two sources of the sudden, unexplained fire.

Survivors reported that they had last seen him crawling through his cabin porthole, his precious manuscript held tightly under his arm. The man who knew too much was officially logged in the disaster list as drowned.

His notebooks and manuscripts drifted away in the ebb and flow of the Red Sea's tides. And seven years later, the wealthy and ruthless arms dealers, unhampered by the spotlight of Albert Londres's unfinished investigation, saw their staggering investment in munitions bear fruit when all of Europe was plunged into war.

Disappearing Dorothy

Judge Jules Forstein telephoned his wife one October evening in 1950 to let her know he'd be delayed at a political banquet. 'I don't expect to be too late,' he said. 'Is everything all right?'

There was a reason for the question. The judge seldom left his wife and children alone because of an incident at the house five years earlier. But on this occasion Dorothy was cheerful and she assured her husband that everything was fine. 'Be sure to miss me,' she said.

Mrs Forstein had lived in a state of panic for five years, dating from the evening of 25 January 1945. That day, after leaving her two children with neighbours she had shopped briefly in a supermarket and then walked home alone to the three-storey house in a Philadelphia suburb. As she entered the house, someone leaped out of the small alcove under the front stairs and attacked her in the darkness. She had time to scream only once.

The police crashed through the front door of the Forstein home to find her lying in a pool of blood. She had a broken jaw, a broken nose, a fractured shoulder and concussion.

There was money and jewellery in the house, but nothing had been taken. The motive was murder, said police. The attacker had entered the house without leaving fingerprints or disturbing the locks on doors and windows. And there was no clue as to how he had left the house, either.

Judge Forstein had an unimpeachable alibi for the time of the attack. And Mrs Forstein had no known enemies. The intruder could have been an enemy of her husband's but months of investigation turned up no suspect.

Though there was a slow physical recovery, Dorothy Forstein never recovered emotionally from the beating. She made a frequent ritual of checking and rechecking the extra locks that had been put on doors and windows. She constantly sought the companionship of relatives and neighbours sometimes during parties she would retreat into deep silence.

But she was getting better, Judge Forstein reassured himself when he returned late from the banquet that evening five years after the attack.

Inside the dimly lit house, the first thing he heard were the screams of his two small children, Edward and Marcy. He found them huddled together in a bedroom, crying convulsively. 'It's mamma,' they told him. 'Something was here and took mamma away.'

Sick with fright, Forstein searched every room of the house. There were her purse, money and keys, but Dorothy Forstein was gone.

Through bursts of tears, Marcy told him what had happened. She had been awakened by terrifying sounds in the night and had run to her mother's bedroom. Through a crack in the door, she saw her mother lying face down on the rug with a shadowy figure crouching over her. 'She looked sick,' the little girl wept.

The intruder had then picked up her mother and thrown her over his shoulder with her head hanging down his back. He saw the child watching and said, 'Go back to sleep. Your mother has been sick, but she'll be all right now.' He went down the stairway carrying Dorothy Forstein, who was dressed only in red silk pyjamas.

When the police arrived, they confessed themselves baffled. There were no fingerprints anywhere, and it seemed incredible to them that any man balancing a woman on his shoulder could have left the house without grasping something for support. Why had no one tried to stop him when he walked down a busy street carrying an unconscious woman in pyjamas? And how did he get into the Forstein home through the multiple locks on the doors and windows?

The police checked every hospital in Philadelphia, as well as rooming houses, rest homes, hotels and the morgue. The search yielded no information about Dorothy.

Whoever had abducted the judge's wife had taken her away for ever. Dorothy Forstein left behind her only the haunting memory of her last words: 'Be sure to miss me.'

Mystery at Wolf's Neck

It was a bitterly cold evening in January 1931 when bus driver Cecil Johnstone saw a fire on a desolate moor at Wolf's Neck between Newcastle upon Tyne and Otterburn in Northumberland. He stopped to investigate. What he saw was almost unbelievable. On fire was the car owned by his boss's daughter, Evelyn Foster. Beside it lay Evelyn, badly burned but still alive.

Johnstone drove her to her home at Otterburn, where she told her parents and the police that she had been attacked by a man who had set fire to her car. She died the following day and left behind her one of the strangest crime stories of the decade. If indeed it was a crime at all . . .

Evelyn Foster was 28 and the daughter of Mr J. J. Foster, who owned a garage at Otterburn. She had her own car, which she ran as a one-cab taxi business.

At 19.00 on 6 January 1931, she arrived home and told her mother that a man who had got out of a car at nearby Elishaw wanted her to drive him to Ponteland, near Newcastle, to catch the bus home. She said the man had looked respectable and gentlemanly when she picked him up at the Percy Arms Hotel.

The next time her mother saw her was when she was brought home dying of burns later that night by her father's bus driver, Johnson. And this is the story she told her mother and a doctor, nurse and policeman who had been called to the house . . .

After she had driven through the village of Belsay, about 8 km (5 miles) from Ponteland, her passenger suddenly asked her to turn back. She had turned round and was driving back when the man hit her in the eye and took over the wheel. He stopped the car at the top of the hill at Wolf's Neck and started 'knocking her about'. He then put her into the back of the car and raped her.

The man then took a bottle or tin out of his pocket and threw something over her. She just 'went up in a blaze'. She then felt a bump as the car was going over rough ground. Evelyn told her mother: 'I was all alight. I do not know how I got out of the car. I lay on the ground and sucked the grass. I was thirsty.'

Her last words were said to have been: 'I have been murdered.' And it really looked as though she had been murdered – until doubts began to surface at the inquest.

To begin with, nobody other than Evelyn saw a stranger in the village that evening. Her father admitted that he had not seen the man. And the owners of the Percy Arms pub, where Evelyn was said to have picked him up, said that no stranger had been in the bar and they had heard no talk about a taxi to Ponteland.

The pathologist who conducted the post mortem on Evelyn, Professor Stuart McDonald, said there were no external injuries on the body apart from the burns. There was no trace or evidence of bruising of the face to suggest that she had been knocked about and there was 'no sign at all' that she had been raped.

Doubts were also cast on Evelyn's suggestion that she and the car had been set on fire before it was driven off the road on to the moor. There were signs of burned heather where the car was found just off the road – but no sign of burned heather by the side of the road itself.

In his summing up the coroner, Mr P. M. Dobbs, told the jury they could rule out suicide. The only two points they had to consider were: Was Evelyn Foster murdered? Or did she set fire to the car to obtain insurance money and set light to herself accidentally?

It took two hours for the jury to reach a verdict. It was: wilful murder on the part of some person or persons unknown.

Later, the police took the unprecedented step of declaring that, in their view, the 'murderer' did not exist. The Chief Constable of Northumberland, Captain Fullarton James, declared in a newspaper interview that the verdict of the inquest was against the weight of evidence and Evelyn Foster had not been murdered.

Gradually, the mystery of Wolf's Neck dropped out of the news – until just over three years later. At the beginning of 1934, a Yorkshire groom, Ernest Brown, was sentenced to death at Leeds Assizes for the murder of his lover's husband. In a 'confession' on the scaffold he is reported to have said either 'ought to burn' or 'Otterburn'. But he died seconds later.

Did Brown murder Evelyn Foster? Or did he know something about her death? The answer is unlikely ever to be known.

Spring-heeled Jack, the Demon of London

There was but one topic on the lips of the people of London in 1838 ... the identity of the mysterious fiend who pounced on young women at night and whose appearance left most of them too terrified even to give a cogent description of their attacker.

At first, tales of this devil-like figure had been treated as hysterical nonsense. But reports, mainly from people crossing Barnes Common in southwest London, continued – and in January 1838 this strange creature received official recognition.

At London's Mansion House the Lord Mayor, Sir John Cowan, read out a letter from a terrified citizen of Peckham describing a demonic figure. Other complaints flooded in from people who until then had been too afraid of ridicule to report their encounters with the creature who had become known as Spring-heeled Jack.

South London barmaid Polly Adams had been savagely attacked while walking across Blackheath. Servant girl Mary Stevens was terrorized on Barnes Common. And an unnamed woman was assaulted in Clapham churchyard. Eighteen-year-old Lucy Scales, a butcher's daughter was attacked in Limehouse. Jane Alsop was almost strangled by the cloaked creature in her own home before her family were able to beat off the attacker.

The description the Alsops gave of the mysterious fiend made him sound inhuman. Jane said: 'His face was hideous, his eyes were like balls of fire, and his hands had icy claws . . .'

Her description was to be echoed repeatedly by other terrified and presumably hysterical victims. But police and public did not dismiss them. Even the Duke of Wellington, although nearly 70, armed himself and went out on horseback to hunt down the monster.

Reports of attacks persisted for several years, not only in London now, but from all parts of the country.

In February 1855 the inhabitants of five south Devon towns awoke to find that there had been a heavy snowfall in which mysterious footprints had appeared overnight. The footsteps ran along the tops of walls, over rooftops, and across enclosed countryside. The hoof-like footprints were attributed by many to Spring-heeled Jack.

In 1870 the army organized a plan to trap him after sentries had been terrorized at their posts by a horrific figure who sprang from the shadows to land on the roofs of their sentry boxes or to slap their faces with icy hands. Their plan failed.

Spring-heeled Jack was last seen in 1804 in Liverpool, leaping up and down the streets from the pavements to the rooftops, only to disappear into the darkness, this time for good.

The World's Last Airship

It was a monster of the skies, a wonder of technology and engineering. The giant airship *Hindenburg* was more than 245 m (800 ft) long and stabilized by a tailfin as high as a ten-storey building. Its four powerful diesel engines gave it the power to cruise effortlessly above the clouds at 36 metres per second (80 mph.). The airship could carry 100 passengers through the atmosphere for a week in a style as opulent as any ocean liner.

When all the 16 bags inside its 22.8 m (75 ft) diameter frame were filled with hydrogen, the airship would wrench itself away from the ground with a lifting force of 239 tonnes (235 tons), enough to raise a modern jumbo jet. Admittedly the properties of hydrogen gas, lighter than the surrounding air, which gave the *Hindenburg* the lift to soar into the sky, brought the risks and dangers of explosion. But with more than a quarter of a century of hard-won experience, the Zeppelin Company was confident that no mishap would endanger their new flagship. They knew that the hydrogen in the gas bags, more than 230,000 cubic metres (7,200,000 cubic feet) of highly inflammable gas, would erupt in a devastating explosion if it was ever ignited. But the design, they said, was flawless. Only an act of God, or deliberate sabotage by a madman, could damage the *Hindenburg*.

And when the *Hindenburg* was consumed in a fire-ball over New Jersey on 6 May 1937, killing 13 of its passengers, 22 of its crew and 1 ground control worker, both the American Goverment and Hitler's Nazi regime conspired to cover up any clues to what may have been the biggest crime in aviation history.

While the fledgling airliners of the 1920s and 1930s were plagued by bad weather and mechanical breakdowns trying to operate services between towns only a few hundred miles apart, the monster airships of Germany appeared regularly over the skyline of Rio de Janeiro and New York.

They had become known simply as Zeppelins, after their brilliant but eccentric designer, the Graf Ferdinand von Zeppelin. Born into a noble Prussian family in 1838, he was an adventurous 23-year-old when he obtained an introduction to US President Abraham Lincoln during the American Civil War and joined the Union Army as a 'guest' cavalry officer.

But the young soldier soon became bored by the slow pace of the war and joined a civilian expedition to explore the sources of the Mississippi River. On a scouting mission at St Paul, Minnesota, he took his first ride in a tethered balloon to survey miles of countryside in one brief flight.

If only balloons could be powered and steered, he enthused, what a perfect gun platform and bombing weapon they would make, soaring safely over the slogging infantry and cavalrymen on the field. His vision of giant balloons or dirigibles as weapons of war never left him but he stayed an earthbound cavalry officer until the end of his military career at the age of 52.

Within a few years of retiring, he had applied for a patent for an airship and began experimenting with the designer, Dr Hugo Eckener, an experienced sailor and meteorologist, at their little workshop near Lake Constance in southern Germany.

By 1909 Zeppelin had formed the world's first airship passenger service, Deutsche Luftschiffahrts Aktien Gesellschaft – DELAG. Operating flights between Berlin, Frankfurt, Hamburg and Dresden, his airships carried 32,750 passengers on 1,600 flights in 5 years without a single accident.

Then came 1914 and the Zeppelins went to war.

The Zeppelin raids over England caused little material damage but they raised panic among the population of London. The sight of the dreaded airships caught in the searchlights, cascading their bombs on to the capital, brought Londoners out into the streets, screaming and shaking their fists impotently in the air.

But within two years the British air aces in their tiny biplane fighters were more than a match for the Zeppelin monsters. In their hydrogen bags the Zeppelins carried the seeds of their own destruction. It took only one hit from the newly developed ZPT tracer bullets coated in burning phosphorus, to turn the airships into flying holocausts.

Graf von Zeppelin died in 1917, just as it was proved that his airships were too vulnerable to gunfire to be machines of war.

But Dr Hugo Eckener struggled through the post-war economic ruin of Germany as chairman of the Zeppelin Company, dreaming of a peaceful future for the airships as transatlantic transports.

In July 1928, the world's most advanced passenger airship, the *Graf Zeppelin*, made its maiden flight on the 90th anniversary of the old Count's birth. Three months later, with 20 passengers aboard, it made its first transatlantic voyage to New York where Eckener and the crew were treated to a ticker-tape welcome. In the next five years of operation on regular services to North and South America, the *Graf Zeppelin* established an unrivalled airship mastery of the skies.

The prestige of this achievement was not lost on the new Nazi masters of Germany. Eckener was not popular with the new regime. Before their rise to power he had made radio broadcasts in Germany condemning their brutality. But with the Nazis controlling the purse strings of German industry, including the Zeppelin Company, he was powerless to stop the traditional black, white and red livery colours of the Zeppelins being repainted with the swastika, the symbol of Hitler and his Nazis.

Eckener, a stubborn 68-year-old, was defiant when he was summoned before Dr Joseph Goebbels, the Propaganda Minister, in 1936 when his newest airship, the biggest, fastest and most powerful, was unveiled.

The airship must be called 'Adolf Hitler', he was told by the Nazi minister. 'No,' Eckener replied. 'I warn you the sight of the swastika on our airships is already provoking hostility when we dock in the United States. If the new airship is called "Adolf Hitler" it will be the target for hatred and sabotage.'

Eckener won the day, but Goebbels decreed that in the German press and on radio the new airship would not be referred to by its Zeppelin Company name, *Hindenburg*. In the Nazi press it was referred to by its works design title – LZ 129.

When the *Hindenburg* began its regular services from Frankfurt to the Lakeheath Naval Air Base in New Jersey it received a rapturous welcome. But as the trickle of persecuted refugees from the Nazis reached a flood-tide on America's shores, Eckener's fears of flaunting the swastika proved to be well founded. In August 1936 more than 100 American demonstrators, posing as celebrating visitors, boarded the German liner *Bremen* as she lay at a pier in New York and sparked off a riotous protest against Hitler's involvement in the Spanish Civil War.

Security was stepped up at the liner berths and at the *Hindenburg*'s hanger across the river at Lakeheath. The American government was concerned by reports that the *Hindenburg* had even been the target of riflemen who had fired potshots at the Zeppelin from atop the Manhattan skyscrapers and from the open fields of New Jersey.

The German ambassador in Washington had received hundreds of threatening phone calls and letters from opponents of the Nazis who were determined to destroy the *Hindenburg* and keep the swastika out of American skies.

Aware of the serious blow to their regime's prestige if the *Hindenburg* was sabotaged, the Sicherheitsddinst, the security élite of Hitler's SS, began to conduct searches of the *Hindenburg*'s hangar in Frankfurt, and the airship itself, before each flight.

On Monday 3 May 1937, Colonel Fritz Erdmann, the new chief of Special Intelligence for the Luftwaffe, was ordered to SS headquarters in Berlin for a briefing on the *Hindenburg* flight due to leave that day.

Erdmann and the two junior officers who were to accompany him in civilian clothes on the flight to America were startled by the briefing given to them by SS Sturmbannführer Major Kurt Hufschmidt. He told them: 'We have reliable information that an attempt will be made to destroy your flight.

The *Hindenburg* in flames

The sabotage will come by bomb, probably after the *Hindenburg* has arrived over American soil. This attack is designed to make the Fatherland look vulnerable in the eyes of our enemies, disloyal Germans, Jews and troublemakers in the United States.'

The ss man also revealed that in March 1935 a bomb had been discovered in the main dining saloon of the *Graf Zeppelin*, hidden underneath a table by one of the passengers. The bomb had been defused safely.

He also told of a Gestapo search of a Frankfurt hotel room for a mysterious passenger who had just arrived from America on a *Hindenburg* flight. The man had travelled on a forged Swedish passport and although he eluded the Gestapo, they searched his room and found detailed technical drawings of both the *Graf Zeppelin* and the *Hindenburg*.

Erdmann was given a rundown on suspect passengers who were making the flight with him. They included: a German couple, both journalists, who were known to have a Jewish writer as a friend, a young photographer from Bonn whose cut-price fare had been arranged by a senior Zeppelin executive since sacked for having Jewish ancestry, a 36-year-old American advertising executive who was known to be a spy for us intelligence, and Joseph Spah, a 35-year-old music hall entertainer from Douglaston, Long Island.

Spah was a comedian and acrobat who travelled on a French passport and had an American wife. But to the humourless ss man he was a suspect because his music hall act, popular in parts of Berlin, was known to contain jokes against people in authority.

At the departure hanger in Frankfurt, all passengers and their luggage were thoroughly searched. Security men confiscated all the young photographer's flashbulbs, fearing they could be used to start a deliberate fire. They also X-rayed a small Dresden china souvenir doll brought on board by Spah.

But the Luftwaffe intelligence officer accepted the assurance of the *Hindenburg* captain, Ernst Lehmann, that the two married journalists were both personal friends who were writing his biography. And Captain Lehmann insisted that the American spy working for the advertising agency had been under close surveillance and posed no threat. The intelligence officer accepted his explanation.

Joseph Spah, according to the captain, was no more than a nuisance. He had brought along a frisky young German shepherd dog which was travelling with him in order to become part of his new act at Radio City Music Hall in New York. The dog travelled in the freight compartment at the rear of the airship and twice Spah had been found unsupervised in the area, away from the authorized passenger lounges. But they accepted his explanation that he must personally feed the nervous young dog during the two-and-a-half-day journey.

Colonel Erdmann reassured the captain: 'Any of our passengers sabotaging the *Hindenburg* on this voyage would be committing suicide. I think the attempt will come after we have moored at Lakeheath. Then it will be the responsibility of the ground staff to ensure the safety of the airship.'

But according to many investigators and historians, a bomb was already on board. An incendiary device, wired to a darkroom photographic timer powered by two small batteries was hidden inside the explosive hydrogen atmosphere of Gas Cell Four, near the tail of the *Hindenburg*.

The *Hindenburg* was due to moor at Lakeheath at 06.00 on 6 May. But the night before it ran into strong headwinds over Newfoundland and the airship radioed it would not arrive until 18.00. The *Hindenburg*'s docking was always made precisely at 06.00 or 18.00 to allow definite working times for the ground crew.

A small reception committee waiting at Lakeheath for the *Hindenburg*'s arrival took advantage of the postponement to go off for dinner in the nearby town of Toms River. They included broadcaster Herbert Morrison, who was preparing to record a commentary on the airship's mooring for the listeners of station WLS in Chicago.

By mid-afternoon on 6 May the *Hindenburg* had passed Long Island sound and the sight of the giant airship with its glittering swastikas brought traffic to a halt in Manhattan. As it crossed the baseball stadium at Ebbet's Field in Brooklyn, the game between the Brooklyn Dodgers and the Pittsburgh Pirates was suspended while players and spectators alike gaped in admiration at the pride of Hitler's Germany.

Just before 16.00 the airship arrived over Lakeheath, but Captain Lehmann set a southerly cruising course to ride out the stormy winds for two hours until the ground crew mustered for his appointed time of arrival.

At 17.22, the *Hindenburg* was being advised by ground control to keep circling ahead of an approaching storm front. And it was then, it is believed, that a timer on the detonator of the fire-bomb hidden in Gas Cell Four was set – for two hours hence.

An hour later Lakeheath radioed: 'Advise landing now' and the airship headed for the airfield. At 19.05 the *Hindenburg* crossed the south fence of the airfield. As 92 US Navy men and 139 civilian workers prepared to reach for the mooring lines which would be dropped from the *Hindenburg* to secure the airship, radio reporter Herbert Morrison could see cheerful passengers at the open promenade deck windows waving at him.

At 19.22 the *Hindenburg* lowered the mooring lines and gave one last burst of her engines to line the airship up with the 61 m (200 ft) mooring tower.

If the airship had been on schedule, all the passengers would have disembarked and it would have been floating at the mooring mast with only a skeleton crew... But the timer on the bomb had been set to the original schedule.

At 19.22 there was a puff of flame and a fire-ball 122 m (400 ft) across erupted from the linen-covered framework of the *Hindenburg*.

Herbert Morrison had been describing the scene as the airship docked:

> What a sight it is ... a thrilling one ... a marvellous sight. The sun is striking the window of the observation deck on the westward side and sparkling like glittering jewels on the background of dark velvet. Oh, oh, oh ... it's burst into flames. Get out of the way please. Oh my, this terrible – it's burning, bursting into flames, it's falling. Oh, this is one of the worst, oh, all the humanity ...

His voice trailed off in tears.

When the film from the newsreel cameras which recorded the fire-ball were processed, it showed that it took only 34 seconds from the first explosion of flame until the glowing framework of the *Hindenburg* hit the ground. The millions of cubic feet of hydrogen had flamed off in less than a minute, although the blaze of engines, fuel oil and framework lasted for hours.

The crew men on the ground, holding the mooring lines underneath the burning giant, scattered and ran for their lives.

One of them, Allen Hagaman, tripped over the rails surrounding the mooring tower and the glowing framework of the airship crashed down on him. He was identified the next day by the scorched remains of his wedding ring.

But in the few seconds as the *Hindenburg* fell from the sky, there were miraculous escapes as passengers and crew leaped from the crashing airship, or simply stayed inside the burning wreckage until it settled on the ground and ran to safety through the white-hot hoops of the *Hindenburg* framework. Joe Spah was one of those who survived. He jumped more than 9 m (30 ft) from the burning airship and, with his acrobat's training, landed apparently unhurt. Luftwaffe intelligence colonel Fritz Erdmann, who had predicted an attack would come after the *Hindenburg* had landed, perished in the flames. Of the 36 passengers, 13 died. Of the 61 crew members, 22 died.

In the commission of inquiry that followed, German experts were invited to join the investigation as 'observers'. Most of the commission's discussions were 'off-the-record' talks between American government officials and high ranking German diplomats.

Documents now filed in the National Archives in Washington show that the American and German technical experts agreed not to consider sabotage as a cause of the disaster – at least in public.

The archives show that senior officers of the American Departments of Commerce and the Interior warned the commission solicitor Mr Trimble Jr that 'a finding of sabotage might be a cause for an international incident, especially on these shores'. The commission ignored a written report by Detective George McCartney of the New York Police Department bomb squad, who analysed the wreckage and reconstructed technical details of a firebomb which he believed had been placed in Gas Cell Four. And the chief of the Luftwaffe, Hermann Goering, ordered the German technical advisers to the commission not to cooperate with any avenue of investigation that hinted at sabotage by any member of the crew.

After a month-long hearing, the commission reached a conclusion backed by both the Americans and Germans. The hydrogen fire-ball had been sparked off, they claimed, by a freak spark of static electricity, an unfortunate phenomenon not seen before and not seen since. Hermann Goering concurred: 'It was an act of God. No one could have prevented it.'

But behind the scenes in Germany, the Gestapo were ruthlessly interrogating the families and friends of every one of the *Hindenburg* crew and passengers. Their suspicions eventually focussed on 25-year-old Eric Spehl. As a rigger on the *Hindenburg* he was one of the crew responsible for checking the gas bags for leaks.

Spehl had been a devout Catholic, never a fervent supporter of the Nazi regime. And he had one great weakness, a passionate love for a divorced woman ten years older than himself who had become his mistress.

Gestapo agents, who checked the gossip with Spehl's neighbours in Frankfurt, found that the young man had gone through a traumatic meeting with his mistress's ex-husband just before the *Hindenburg*'s last voyage. The man had come to Spehl's flat. He was an artist, he was haggard and half crazed with fear. He was on the run from the Gestapo and needed money to escape.

Spehl gave him all the money he had ... and then tipped off the Gestapo. The Nazi torturers arrested the artist and crushed his fingers one by one in a vice until the bones showed through his knuckles. Spehl was reported to be infuriated by the sight and still seething with anger when he boarded the fatal *Hindenburg* flight.

The Gestapo searchers in Frankfurt ripped Spehl's apartment to pieces. They could find no sign of his mistress, who had fled the city. And they could find no trace of Eric's beloved new gadget for his photographic darkroom, his two-hour timer.

Neither could they interrogate Eric Spehl. He died, horribly burned, in the emergency field hospital set up at Lakeheath, beside the glowing embers of the world's last great airship.

Chapter
Two

Crimes
of Our Time

The Computer as Crook

The unsolved crime is usually hailed as the perfect crime. It is a misnomer. More often than not, a crime remains unsolved thanks to a combination of poor planning, coupled with good luck on the criminal's part and sometimes helped by a faulty police investigation. The really perfect crime is never reported. It remains unsolved because it is unrecognized and undetected as a piece of villainy.

And in the criminal's quest for illegal perfection, many have found a willing new accomplice who never gets nervous about being caught and punished, who has no criminal record, leaves no fingerprints and never demands a share of the loot... The computer, an electronic brain without scruples or morals, is the perfect partner in crime.

At the beginning of the 1980s it was estimated that there were 300,000 large computers at work in businesses in the United States, Europe and Japan, juggling enormous amounts of cash and commodities every week. Unlike human clerks and bank tellers, with all their frailties and temptations, computers never get their sums wrong and do not possess sticky fingers to dip into the till.

The decision of the almighty computer is final, whether it is sending a demand for payment to a customer who is vainly disputing the bill or releasing vast amounts of hard cash on invoices it has cleared for payment. The computer is above suspicion.

Small wonder then that it has not taken long for criminals to realize the potential of getting the computer on their side. For the computer's infallibility is a double-edged sword. If crooked information is fed in at the start of the process, impeccably crooked instructions are produced at the other end and no one doubts the orders the machine gives them.

That is what electronic whizz-kid Jerry Schneider discovered when he became a millionaire by defrauding the master computer of the Pacific Bell Telephone Company in Los Angeles in 1972. Schneider's crime is still unsolved, only he knows exactly how he fooled the electronic brain. The computer records reveal nothing.

The 21-year-old high school graduate was struggling to form his own telephone equipment supply business when he discovered secret codes which allowed him to tap into the computer controlling the stocks in the warehouse of Pacific Bell in California. Using his own modified computer terminal at home, Schneider persuaded the electronic stock controller he was a legitimate installation contractor for the phone company and he began to order costly wiring and exchange equipment from the warehouse.

The computer accepted his instructions and despatched its expensive goods to locations all over Los Angeles, often to the pavements beside manhole covers where the delivery drivers dumped the bulky crates of electronics, assuming another crew would arrive later to install the equipment. They did not wait to see this operation.

Schneider, with his own truck painted to resemble the phone company vehicles, would hijack the equipment, then return home to tap into the computer once more and give it orders to wipe the whole transaction from its electronic memory.

With his giant rival supplying all his equipment free, Schneider's business boomed until he foolishly refused a pay rise to one of his employees, who then tipped off the police. Even after his arrest officials of the phone company refused to believe that Schneider had milked their warehouse of $1 million worth of equipment in less than a year. If their computer insisted there was nothing missing, they were not prepared to argue with it. Only after police investigators physically went round the warehouse, totalling up the stocks with old-fashioned pen and paper, did the phone company admit their losses.

But Schneider spent only a few weeks in prison. The phone company dropped charges against him after he gave them a secret briefing on the electronic loopholes in their system.

On his release from prison Schneider set himself up in a new business, as one of America's highest paid computer security consultants, revealing the secrets of his unsolved crime for fat fees and searching the electronic brains of his clients' machines for similar loopholes which can let crooked computer operators steal by remote control.

As Jerry Schneider said:

> 'Many of my clients had already been robbed blind without realising it. They had lost millions of dollars through computer manipulation and the culprits can never be traced because the electronic evidence of their crimes has been wiped out.
>
> Who needs to take the risk of leaping over a bank counter with a sawn-off shotgun when they can sit in the comfort of their own home and rob the bank of even more money just by using a telephone and a computer terminal?'

In the United States, FBI officials estimate the average haul in armed bank robberies amounts to $10,000 a time. But the average electronic bank fraud is enriching crooks by $500,000 a time with only a tiny percentage of the microchip embezzlements uncovered and solved.

In 1980 it was estimated that unsolved computer crime in the US and

Common Market countries was producing a haul of £200 million a year and growing fast.

New York police are still searching for the amiable young man who pulled off a childishly simple computer fraud when he signed a loan agreement with a local bank for $20,000 to buy himself a new car. The bank's computer paid the car dealer and the vehicle ownership papers were safely stored in the bank's filing cabinet as security for the loan. A few days later the proud new driver received his loan repayment book, with 12 monthly coupons to be processed by the computer as he coughed up the instalments over the next year.

The young man ignored the first 11 coupons and posted the twelfth with a money order to the computer when his first instalment was due. Then he waited.

There is nothing as blind as an infallible machine. The computer recognized only the magnetic ink code on the coupon as the twelfth and final instalment. With unfailing efficiency it sent the car driver a glowing letter thanking him for paying off the loan. It also posted him the ownership documents to the car and a printed assurance that he now had an outstanding credit rating at the bank.

More than a month later a puzzled bank official went to visit the new customer's address in search of an overdue instalment. His apartment was empty and the gleaming Cadillac had already been sold to a local car dealer who had happily, and legally, accepted the computer's decision that the car was paid for and owned by the young driver who wanted a cash sale to pay for a 'heart operation' for his ailing father. The mysterious driver was never traced despite strenuous efforts to do so.

Another stunningly easy fraud netted $350,000 in one week for the pretty blonde 'divorcée' who opened her own account with $200 when she arrived at a bank in Miami, Florida. She was planning to buy herself a luxury home near the beach, she explained, just as soon as her divorce settlement came through from her husband. The bank happily issued her with a chequebook and a book of paying-in slips with her own personalized account number printed in one corner in magnetic ink characters.

They never noticed her stop at the counter as she left, when she scooped up a handful of blank paying-in slips in a tray for the convenience of customers who had forgotten to bring their own personalized books.

Somehow (and no one has ever publicly explained the mystery) the young blonde printed her own account number in magnetic ink at the bottom left hand corner of all the blank slips. A few days later she reappeared at the bank and slipped her own specially doctored paying-in slips to the tray at the counter.

For the next five days, busy customers who had forgotten to bring their pre-printed paying-in slips reached for the apparently blank forms on the tray and paid their earnings and savings into the bank. The computer was programmed to direct the pen-and-ink slips into a storage basket for manual sorting. But it instantly recognized the magnetic ink numbers and faithfully credited all the money to the divorcée's account. When she returned a few days later she found her 'dream home' and she was accompanied by a burly male friend with a security attaché case.

She cleaned out all but a few hundred dollars from the account, scooping up a kitty of £150,000 which had been built up for her by unsuspecting customers who kicked up hell at the end of the month when their statements showed their hard-earned cash had not been credited to their accounts. The blonde and her friend were never seen again.

A more ambitious crook used his innocent girl friend as his unwitting accomplice when he robbed the computer of a bank in Washington, DC, in 1981.

The dapper middle-aged businessman boasted that he was a furniture manufacturer from San Francisco and would soon be bringing new jobs to Washington when he had found a suitable site for his new factory. The bank welcomed him as a potentially valuable customer when he opened his account and told them to expect a very large deposit to follow from his company account in San Francisco.

True to his word, a few days later the San Francisco bank made an electronic transfer of $2 million to Washington. The furniture manufacturer promptly presented himself at the bank, collected the money in a cashier's draft and set off 'looking for development land'. When he failed to reappear, and when the hard cash never arrived from San Francisco, bank investigators started to track down the source of the computer transfer of money.

After months of searching they finally traced the electronic message to one computer terminal at the bank in San Francisco, operated by a group of three female employees who all denied any knowledge of the transfer. But they did tell the investigators that a fourth woman had left her job at the bank only a few weeks before, broken-hearted after an unhappy love affair.

The woman was traced and told in tears how her middle-aged boyfriend had promised to marry her after returning home briefly to Washington to assure his friends and family that he had made his fortune in California. The boyfriend was a great fun-loving practical joker, she explained. He had even persuaded her to send a telex to a bank in Washington crediting him with $2 million as a prank to impress his friends and relations.

The telex message was the only souvenir the bank has left of the fraudster. Their computer had paid out without the need to see the cash or count laboriously through piles of crisp banknotes as a bored, under-paid human teller would have to do. To the computer a burst of electronic bleeps over a telephone line was as good as money in the bank.

But the prize for the most sought after computer conman of the new electronic age must surely go to the New York genius who was able tap his way into a municipal computer which controlled no cash, no valuable stocks, no sensitive information.

The AM Tote 300 computer at Belmont racetrack is just an adding machine which is supposed to total up the amount of money bet on each day's racing to an accuracy within a single cent.

Since revenue from the Tote betting tax contributes to the income of the City of New York, that figure is a matter of record. Each day New York newspapers publish the figure. It is simply a statistic which varies each day according to the amount of business done at the racetrack.

The final sum from the impartial computing machine is taken for granted as accurate even by the down-to-earth businessmen of the Mafia. And that daily betting total is the heart of the Mafia's illegal bookmaking enterprise, the numbers racket. The Mafia's persuasive street salesmen offer a daily lottery ticket where a gambler can choose any three digits which he or she thinks will form the vital last three numbers of that day's betting total at Belmont.

The chances of getting the numbers right are 999 to 1. But the organizers pay out odds of only 500 to 1, making a profit on half the $3 million New Yorkers bet on the racket each week.

On 30 September 1980, a crowd of 20,000 gamblers spent a day at the races and bet a total of $3,339,916. The following day the Mafia bookies paid out $250,000 to lucky holders who had chosen the winning number as number 916.

A few days later the auditors handling the racetrack's accounts announced that the computer had mistotalled the amount by $3 and altered the last three figures to 919. The Mafia bookies who had already paid out on the earlier figure, made the splendidly warm-hearted gesture of paying out again on the new total to enhance their reputation as nice honest guys to do business with.

Then the auditors completed an overhaul of the Tote 300 computer and checked its totals against actual cash deposits paid into the bank. In six months the Tote 300 had given the wrong betting total 80 times. Its simple adding machine memory had been accepting any last three numbers fed into it by a crooked computer operator who clicked its electronic register to any numbers he chose.

The Mafia had been conned out of $20 million.

A Sadistic Revenge

'**O**nly a few evil sadists will carry with them to their graves the knowledge of whether her body was alive or dead when they set her on fire.'

The words come from the man known as the White Rat of Uganda: self-styled 'Major' Bob Astles, the British acolyte of one of the most barbarous tyrants the world has ever seen, Idi Amin. They refer to a gentle old woman with dual Israeli-British citizenship who unwittingly became caught up in the now legendary Israeli commando rescue of a hijacked aeroplane and its hostages at Uganda's Entebbe Airport in 1976.

Dora Bloch, aged 73, was one of 105 hostages freed by the bullet in one of the most daring, audacious military swoops of its kind in modern, peacetime history. Freed, tragically, only for an instant ... because she was hurt during the armed sortie and was left behind to recuperate in a Ugandan hospital.

The Ugandan capitulation afer the Entebbe raid was absolute. So, it soon became clear, was Amin's lust for revenge. And the pathetically frail object of that revenge appears to have been Mrs Dora Bloch.

It was only later that clues began to emerge about what really happened to this grandmother, whose only wish when she boarded the 747 Jumbo jet was to see again her relatives in Tel Aviv.

In 1980 a British journalist smuggled a message into Uganda's grim Luzira Prison, where Amin's British aide Astles was being held, following the flight of the tyrant and the country's liberation by troops sent in by neighbouring Tanzania.

In a letter smuggled out to the newsman, Mike Parker, Astles told how he had tracked down Mrs Bloch's grave at a time when Amin was denying to the world that his secret police had slain her.

Rumours in the country had been rife that Mrs Bloch had been tortured to death in the notorious State Research Bureau outside Kampala, along with thousands of others – enemies real and imagined – who had simply vanished after being abducted there.

Astles, however, told Parker in his smuggled letter that he confronted Amin after discovering Mrs Bloch's jungle grave. He wrote:

'Then, all hell let loose, I was summoned to see Amin – and he was in one of his most horrendous rages. His eyes glared with terrible anger.

I knew I was going to be in trouble for asking questions, but I wasn't going to back down. I said to Amin. "Bring me the body of Dora Bloch."

And then I was brought down to earth. It was flung at me, by Amin, that I had had a part in her killing. How could I have done? At the time, I was on leave in London.

I came back to Uganda because it was the only life I knew. And I vowed to Mrs Bloch's niece, Mrs Ruth Hammond, in a meeting at her London home, that I would discover what had happened to her aunt.

The truth is that I was working with Israeli Intelligence – but nobody knew at the time.'

'The truth' as propounded by Astles may be anything but fact. Nevertheless, documents recovered since Amin's overthrow – some of them from the so-called State Research Bureau – reveal that Mrs Bloch was dragged screaming from Mulago Hospital, Kampala, after being admitted there as a patient only hours after the successful commando raid on Entebbe Airport.

It was later claimed that she had been taken there for treatment after being unknowingly left behind by the Israeli troops. But subsequent statements from witnesses suggest that she was far too weak to travel and, for the sake of the safety of the rest of the liberated hostages, she was left behind in the hope that Amin would allow her to be treated and then released on her recovery.

It was not to be. Astles said:

'She was a suffering, pathetic old woman. But the State Research police were incensed by the Israeli attack. They wanted immediate retribution.

I have been told many stories about her death. But I was informed by a member of State Research that she was kicked and pummelled to the ground after being dragged from her hospital bed.

Her body, I was told, was finally set ablaze. And only a few evil sadists know whether she was alive or dead when they set her on fire.'

Astles added, chillingly:

'Animals from the State Research Bureau were openly bragging about the white woman they had killed. They were boasting of how she had been buried after being beaten and burned and it was an easy job to find her unmarked grave – at a place called Nakapinyi.

I arranged to go there with a friend, but somehow our secret got out. My friend was thrown into jail. And I, too, would have been imprisoned by Amin if I'd made any attempt to get to the body.

Despite my demands, Amin refused to acknowledge that Mrs

Idi Amin

Bob Astles

Bloch had been killed on Ugandan soil. He kept telling the outside world that the 'missing' Mrs Bloch was being searched for. But all along he knew the truth.

I think, in all honesty, that he was ashamed that his State Research Bureau had killed her. He would never admit that she died the horrible death that she did on his orders. And, despite my demands, he adamantly refused to let anyone else try to appease her mourning family by finding her body.'

Mrs Bloch's grave was, in fact, finally unearthed by Ugandan police in May, 1979. Her bones were identified by top Israeli pathologist Dr Maurice Rogoff and flown to her homeland for burial. A grave had been prepared for her in Jerusalem by one of her sons, Bertram, and at last she was laid to rest.

Bob Astles told reporter Mike Parker: 'The sorry way in which Dora Bloch died will serve forever as an indictment of Idi Amin. Her killing was needless – a sordid act of revenge by people against whom this fragile person was totally defenceless.'

Piracy 20th Century Style

There is nothing romantic about pirates. In the days of sail they were bloodthirsty killers. In the present day they are just as deadly, just as ruthless, just as merciless. The main difference is that in the days of Blackbeard and Captain Kidd, pirates usually ended their careers on the gallows or in Davy Jones's locker. In the 20th century, however, they get away. Their crimes almost always remain unsolved.

Piracy has become a renewed menace around the world, the most blighted regions being the Caribbean, the West African coast and the Far East. Many ships leaving Singapore for the open seas now frequently take on armed guards to protect them from attack by pirates, who mainly operate from nearby islands with high-speed boats.

In the Philippines, the British captain of a container ship dropped anchor to ride out a storm, and thought he and his crew were safe from danger. But under cover of darkness pirates drew alongside in a fishing boat, threw up grappling hooks and hauled themselves on board the container ship as it lay in Manila Bay. The bandits forced their way to the captain's cabin, pointed a gun at his neck and demanded money. Captain Arthur Dyason refused, and moved as if to parry the gun. The pirates opened fire and the captain died.

A horrifying massacre was carried out by pirates in the Tawitawi Islands, about 500 miles north of Manila. The passenger craft *Nuria* had dropped anchor in a calm bay when two crewmen and two stowaways jumped the crew and passengers. Wielding weapons taken from the armoury, they herded everyone to one side of the ship and stripped them of their valuables. Then they opened fire. In a hail of shots 11 people were killed – then callously thrown overboard. Panic ensued and 20 others dived into the sea and were drowned.

Meanwhile the four pirates transferred to two fishing vessels manned by accomplices. Twenty people survived the ordeal, and the pirates, thought to be natives of the region, were never caught.

In 1981 the International Maritime Bureau was established at Barking, Essex, to deal with and collate evidence of crimes committed at sea. Many of the cases the bureau deals with involve insurance fraud. But increasingly, cases of piracy are reported to the investigators. In one of its first reports, the bureau stated with alarm that fierce tribesmen armed with knives and poison-tipped arrows were hired to protect ships from pirates off West Africa.

But it is the Caribbean that is, as ever, the world centre of piracy. In five years, between 1977 and 1982, it was estimated that 1,500 people had been killed by pirates.

The yacht *Belle Esprit* limped into Nassau in the Bahamas with 50 bullet holes in the hull. The captain, Austin Evans, had beaten off an attack from five speed-boats and was eventually rescued by a police spotter plane. Within weeks, pirates raided three sailing boats heading for the Bahamas. They threatened the lives of those on board and robbed them of cash and supplies.

William and Pat Kamemer of Fort Myers, Florida, were murdered when they stumbled across an ocean drug transfer in the Exumas Islands. Walter Falconer and a companion vanished without trace along with their yacht, *Polyner III*, in the 76-mile stretch between Bimini and the Florida coast. After relatives offered a reward word filtered back that both men had been killed and the yacht hijacked to South America.

Peter Beamborough and Michael Collesta fought off four attacking boats near the Williams Islands. They reported afterwards that they sailed their 12-m (40-ft) yawl *Snowbound* to safety in a hail of gunfire. British businessman Michael Crocker died aboard his 9-m (30-ft) yacht *Nyn*, strangled by an armed intruder.

The reason for most of these attacks is the booming and seemingly unstoppable drugs trade. Whereas the currency of the pirates was once gold, it is now marijuana, cocaine and heroin. The route is from South America, through the Caribbean islands to the Florida coast. Mother ships carrying up to 62,000 tonnes (60,000 tons) of marijuana have been seen anchored outside territorial waters, waiting for darkness and the arrival of dozens of small vessels to transfer the cargo to hidden inlets and covers. Some victims have unexpectedly witnessed drug transfers at sea. Others have been attacked and killed, so that their vessels can be used as drug carriers.

In the Cayman Islands the police chief advertised six aircraft for sale – all confiscated from smugglers. He said: 'It doesn't stop the trade. It simply means that more yachts and planes will be stolen to replace them.'

The Colombian drug network is held responsible for most of the sea attacks, but many of the islanders are joining in the pirate operation.

Grafton Iffel, head of the Bahamas CID said: 'There are 700 small islands spread over 100,000 square miles. With limited resources it is an area impossible to control.'

American yachting magazines now openly warn readers: 'Take weapons with you – the bigger the better. Display them when other boats come near. Link up with fellow yachtsmen in harbours and buy the best radio equipment you can afford.'

Captain Mike Green who sailed off the Florida coast for more than 20 years, said:

'Fear is replacing leisure here. Nobody listens to fabulous fishing stories any more. The talk is of bullets across the bow and high-speed runs for safety.

The message to yachtsmen who want to fulfil a life's ambition by sailing these waters is simply – don't. It is no longer safe. These seas belong to the smugglers and the pirates.'

Double Dealing at the Dogs

The most spectacular swindle in the history of greyhound racing was pulled off at London's White City track on 8 December 1945. The perpetrators, who were never caught, got away with more than £100,000, a fortune at the time.

The swindle became apparent to the race fans as they watched the last event of the day. The second favourite, Fly Bessie, led at the first bend, closely followed by Jimmy's Chicken. Then, to the amazement of the 16,000 crowd, the dogs began to swerve drunkenly and lose ground. One by one, they started stumbling ... all except the rank outsider, a white hound called Bald Truth. He streaked home 15 lengths ahead of the second dog, with the favourite, Victory Speech, trailing in fourth.

No one was more amazed than Bald Truth's owner, Colonel B. C. 'Jock' Hartley, wartime director of the Army Sports Board. The dog had only been brought in as a late substitute and his £2 bet on it was prompted more by his heart than his head. He sat speechless as fans shouted and growled and track officials delayed making the official announcements. But there was nothing they could do. Number 4 went up in lights; Bald Truth the winner. Bets would be paid.

As far as Scotland Yard was concerned, however, the affair was far from over. Chief Inspector Robert Fabian was called in to investigate the coup, which had followed a series of minor frauds at tracks around the country. Slowly the pieces of the puzzle were fitted into place. The swindlers had used a dope called cholecretone, untraceable in pre-race examinations, but which had an alcoholic effect as the dogs heated up during a race.

Investigators decided that the culprit had crept into a disused kennel used to store straw and timber. Then, when all eyes were on the track during the penultimate race, he had crawled out, fed drugged pieces of fish to all the dogs except Bald Truth – the only white dog in the field – and returned to his kennel until the coast was clear. Meanwhile the rest of the gang were placing bets with bookies all over the country and on the course, bringing the price down from 33-1 to 11-2 by the start.

But that was all renowned sleuth Fabian of the Yard could discover. Despite the Greyhound Racing Association's offer of a £1,000 reward, the culprits were never caught.

A Fatal Flight

Two planes carrying 116 passengers mysteriously vanished in the Andes – and investigators believe both craft may have been hijacked.

Saeta Airlines Flight 11, with 59 passengers on board, left Quito, Ecuador, on 15 August 1976 on its 45-minute flight to the mountain city of Cuenca. It vanished without trace.

Two years later Saeta Flight 11 left with 57 people bound once again for

Cuenca. It passed over the same relay station as its 1976 namesake then vanished. Intensive searches found no signs of the aircraft or their passengers. But at a special hearing in Quito, five farmers and a teacher gave sworn statements that they saw the second flight suddenly veer from its normal southerly course and head north-east.

Major Carlos Serrano, president of Saeta, one of Ecuador's three domestic airlines, supported the theory that the two Vickers Viscount planes had been hijacked. He said drug smugglers may have been involved. 'They are the perfect planes for them,' he said 'They fly long distances, land on short runways and with the seats removed hold up to 12,000 pounds of cargo.'

Searches for the two planes involved the Ecuadorean Air Force and army patrols, a United States Air Force C-130 search plane and a helicopter with sophisticated laser reconnoitring devices. None of the searches were successful. And Commander Reinaldo Lazo, the United States Military Liaison Chief, said the C-130 crew had reached no conclusions after either of the week-long searches.

James Kuykendall, the Ecuador representative of the United States Drug Enforcement Administration, said his agency had found names of people with narcotics trafficking records on the passenger lists of the missing aircraft. He said his agency had no idea what had happened to the flights.

Saeta's Major Serrano, however, is more certain. He believes the passengers were pressed into service harvesting marijuana. The missing included 74 men, 36 women and 6 children – ranging from farm workers to doctors and lawyers.

Guillermo Jaramillo, a Quito lawyer whose 39-year-old son Ivan disappeared on the second flight, organized a committee of the grieving families to probe the mystery. Together with Saeta, they offered a $325,000 reward for information – without success.

Chapter Three

Crimes
of Avarice

Conviction Without the Corpse

Life as the wife of a high-powered newspaper executive gave Muriel McKay all the trappings of suburban luxury – elegance a million miles removed from the street-wise world of the popular press in which her husband had made it to the top. Her world revolved around a genteel neighbourhood where every home had been built with the wealthy in mind and through whose letter-boxes you would hardly expect to find the daily diet of sin, sex and sensation which was the trademark of husband Alick's downmarket journals of mass-appeal. But on the evening of Monday 29 December 1969, the McKays' world was turned, ruthlessly and without warning, upside down ...

Alick McKay, number two to newspaper tycoon Rupert Murdoch and deputy chairman of the huge-circulation *News of the World,* returned home shortly before 20.00. From the outside, everything looked normal at St Mary House in Arthur Road, Wimbledon, south-west London. It was only after he had rung the doorbell a second time and discovered that the front door was unlocked – alarming in itself since the couple had agreed to take special care following a burglary a few months previously – that he began to realize that something was seriously wrong.

His worst suspicions were confirmed as he stepped into the hallway. Muriel's black handbag was lying open with its contents strewn half-way up the flight of stairs; the telephone had been hurled to the floor; on the hall table was an opened tin of plasters, a bale of thick twine and a rusty, woodenhandled meat-cleaver. Instinctively, Alick picked up the cleaver and raced upstairs, yelling his wife's name, fearing the intruder or intruders were still in the house.

But Muriel McKay, and whoever else had invaded the family home, had gone. Within minutes, Alick, trying to remain calm, discovered that several items of jewellery, including an eternity ring, a gold and pearl pendant, three bracelets and an emerald brooch, and a small amount of money were missing from Muriel's handbag. His mind racing, Alick ran to a neighbour's to see if anyone had heard or seen what had happened. No one had, and from the house next door he phoned the police.

In similar cases the police approach is generally low-key at the outset. Every possibility has to be examined and, in most cases, the most tangible one

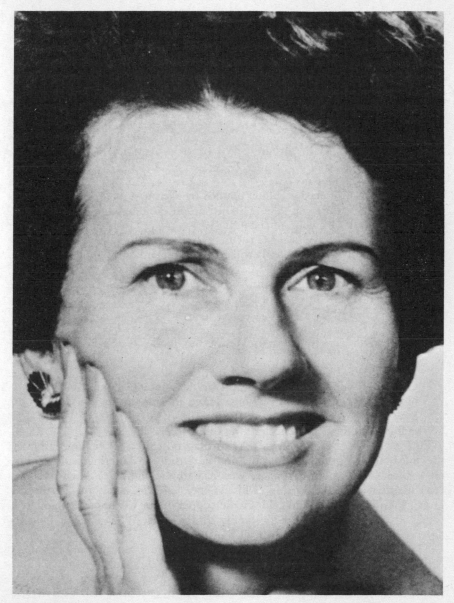

Muriel McKay

is that the person missing has put himself or herself on the missing persons list voluntarily – by simply walking out. And, in an overwhelming number of cases, if there is a culprit to be found, then it is more often than not the spouse who is 'left behind'.

But any thoughts that this was such a case were soon dispelled when, at 01.15 on Tuesday 30 December, the telephone rang at St Mary House. A detective who answered the call beckoned Alick to take the phone as he hurriedly picked up an extension. This was the chilling conversation that followed . . .

> Caller: This is Mafia Group 3. We are from America. Mafia M3. We have your wife.
>
> McKay: You have my wife?
>
> Caller: You will need a million pounds by Wednesday.
>
> McKay: What are you talking about? I don't understand.
>
> Caller: Mafia. Do you understand?
>
> McKay: Yes, I have heard of them.
>
> Caller: We have your wife. It will cost you one million pounds.
>
> McKay: That is ridiculous. I haven't got anything like a million.
>
> Caller: You had better get it. You have friends. Get it from them. We tried to get Rupert Murdoch's wife. We couldn't get her, so we took yours instead.
>
> McKay: Rupert Murdoch?
>
> Caller: You have a million by Wednesday night or we will kill her. Understand?
>
> McKay: What do I do?
>
> Caller: All you have to do is wait for the contact. That is for the money. You will get instructions. Have the money or you won't have a wife. We will contact you again.

The line went dead as the caller rang off.

Further evidence arrived with the morning post, in a letter sent 12 hours previously from Tottenham, north London. Inside, in faltering handwriting on a piece of blue, lined paper, was a pathetic message. Alick McKay recognized at once the writing of his wife: 'Please do something to get me home. I am blindfolded and cold. Please cooperate for I cannot keep going. I think of you constantly and the family and friends. What have I done to deserve this treatment? Love, Muriel.'

The Muriel McKay case had begun to escalate into a major investigation. And with it came the attendant media 'circus'. As the McKay family closed ranks in the house at Arthur Road, one story upon which the press pack thrived was a call to Gerard Croiset, the world-famous Dutch clairvoyant who counted among his more spectacular successes the accurate pinpointing of the graves of murdered schoolchildren in Britain's notorious Moors Murders case. Croiset's unique powers enabled him to point to an area on a map which was, although largely ignored by police at the time, to prove of great significance: the border of Essex and Hertfordshire, some 40 miles outside London.

By the time a full week had elapsed, however, the police, who by then had a 30-strong team of detectives working full-time on the investigation, were still perplexed. Not one positive lead had emerged, despite the usual combing of underworld contacts and a check of hundreds of jewellers to discover whether Mrs McKay's missing possessions had been 'fenced'. The newspapers were running headline stories such as 'The Case That Does Not Add Up', and the crank callers and con-men, one of whom was later fined for trying to extort money from Alick McKay, were hampering what few inquiries could reasonably be made.

By 6 January every Metropolitan Police officer had been issued with a full description of Muriel McKay, her photograph had been posted on 'Wanted and Missing' boards at police stations throughout the country, Interpol had been alerted and a special watch was being kept on all entry points to Australia, the McKays' country of origin.

The breakthrough came a fortnight later. A large envelope posted from Wood Green, north London, contained another letter from Muriel, which read:

> 'I am deteriorating in health and spirit. Please cooperate. Excuse writing, I'm blindfolded and cold. Please keep the police out of this and cooperate with the gang giving Code M3 when telephoning you. The earlier you get the money the quicker I may come home or you will not see me again. Darling can you act quickly. Please, please keep the police out of this if you want to see me. Muriel.'

Also in the envelope was the ransom demand for one million pounds.

Three more telephone calls from the so-called M3 group came the following day. As the kidnap gang issued a series of demands, rendezvous points and instructions, Alick McKay desperately pleaded for some form of proof that his wife was still alive.

The gang responded with a further letter, accompanied by three pieces of material – one from the green woollen two-piece outfit Mrs McKay had been wearing, another from her black top coat and a snip of leather cut from one of her shoes. From the fourpenny stamp on the envelope, police scientific experts were able to remove a thumb-print. It did not belong to Mrs McKay. Much later it was matched to the thumb of a man called Arthur Hosein.

Police began to plot the ransom handover. It was to be made in two stages – apparently of £500,000 a time. But only £300 of the money, borrowed for the operation from Alick McKay, was to be genuine. The rest would be duds.

A series of attempted drops of the 'ransom money' followed over the next few days, resulting in some farcical mix-ups. The tolerance of the kidnap gang was wearing thin. And to the police, the gang's indecisive, amateurish handling of the actual ransom forced them to consider the possibility that the kidnappers were 'first-timers'.

The crucial day was Friday 5 February. A final call came from the gang: 'If you do not drop the money, she will be dead. You must trust M3. We deal with high-powered telescopic rifles. Anyone trying to interfere with the cases – we will let them have it.'

An elaborate plan was agreed whereby, after a supposedly monitored journey by tube-train and taxi, the money was to be dropped off by a hedge close to a garage on the Bishop's Stortford road in Hertfordshire. This time the plan went like clockwork, with police 'staking out' the drop, ready to swoop on whoever collected the ransom.

It transpired that no one did. But the police, mercifully, had their first stroke of luck. A Volvo 144 car – registration number XGO 994G – was spotted twice circling the drop-off point. It was the same vehicle that had turned up on an earlier, abortive delivery run. It belonged to Arthur Hosein.

Hosein, a Trinidad-born immigrant tailor, had, he believed, finally found his niche in English society when, in 1967, he purchased for the modest price of £14,000 Rooks Farm in Stocking Pelham, Hertfordshire. Two years after he moved in with his German-born wife Else, his younger brother Nizamodeen joined them. They were, from the start, a bizarre family, constantly at odds with their rural neighbours.

Villagers remember how quickly Arthur became known as 'King Hosein', because of his incredible arrogance and boasts that it was his intention to become 'an English gentleman and a millionaire'. It was patently clear, even then, that he exerted an eerie, Svengali-like influence over his younger, easily-dominated brother. Arthur would talk expansively of his 'estate' – and if Nizamodeen ever dared remind him of the more mundane reality of failing, neglected Rooks Farm, he would be severely castigated.

Despite his Walter Mitty existence, however, Arthur did realize that his dreams of vast wealth were unlikely to be fulfilled were he simply to rely on his ailing smallholding. Then, two months before Christmas 1969, an idea for actually making that million took root in the brothers' minds.

They were watching television when they saw what they believed to be the answer to all their problems: the affluence of Rupert Murdoch. The press tycoon was a guest on the popular David Frost show, talking of his newspapers' involvement in the exposé of the notorious Christine Keeler sex-and-politics scandal. References were made to Murdoch's beautiful blonde

Arthur and Nizamodeen Hosein

wife Anna, as well as the sort of enormous sums his newspaper, the *News of the World*, was willing to part with in exchange for exclusive stories.

A crude, but seemingly foolproof plan was hatched to abduct Anna Murdoch and hold her to ransom for one million pounds. The plan was put into operation just after the Christmas break. Only it was Muriel McKay, the wife of Murdoch's second-in-command, who became the target, purely by accident when the bungling brothers got the addresses of the two executives mixed-up; they followed Rupert Murdoch's Rolls-Royce which was being used by the McKays while Murdoch was away.

At 08.00 on the misty morning of 6 February, a squad of 20 detectives, armed with a search warrant obtained by Chief Superintendent Smith of Wimbledon police in west London, walked up the short driveway to the house at Rooks Farm in Stocking Pelham. They told Arthur Hosein's wife Else, who answered the door, that they were making inquiries about a cache of jewellery which had been stolen in London 39 days previously.

At first, Arthur Hosein remained cool enough to cast doubt in the searchers' minds as to whether he might, indeed, be their man. His wife, who seemed understandably irritated at having so many men trample around her home, also showed no signs of stress. And Arthur himself, when questioned about the missing jewellery, calmly replied: 'I know nothing. I earn over £150 a week. I do not deal in stolen property. You can look where you like.'

Look the detectives did. Methodically, painstakingly they began their search of Rooks Farm. It was only a matter of minutes before a vital shred of evidence – the first of many – came to light. From an upstairs bedroom, a young detective constable emerged with some blue and yellow slips of paper, cut into the shape of flowers for the Hosein children, which were identical to scraps found at one of the earlier ransom drop-offs.

A writing pad, on which could be made out the indentations of words that had been written on a previous page, was taken away. Experts later matched the indentations to one of the pathetic letters Muriel McKay had been forced to write by her captors. More sinisterly, a shotgun, the double-barrels of which had been sawn down in the fashion now favoured by criminals, was discovered. Moreover, it had recently been fired. Later, a key witness was to say he had heard a single shot ring out from the direction of Rooks Farm several days earlier.

The mounting evidence then took a nightmarish turn – one which was to lead to the most grisly of theories and seal forever the mystery which surrounds the Muriel McKay case. Police discovered a billhook, recently used to slaughter animals, in the farmhouse. At the time of this sinister discovery, Arthur Hosein casually commented: 'I borrowed it from a farmer friend. I wanted to chop up a calf. It was Nizam [Arthur's pet name for his brother] who did the chopping. We fed it to the dogs and put the bones and head with the rubbish.'

The information was not, perhaps, sinister in itself. But allied to the fact that the Hosein brothers had recently sold a number of pigs at market, and that traces of bone were found in the fire at their house, police began to ponder the dreadful theory that Muriel McKay may have been murdered ... and then fed to the pigs.

Had they ever been able to trace the livestock the brothers sold, they might have found the traces of cortisone – a drug Mrs McKay had been prescribed by the family doctor – which would have proved the unthinkable. But the body of Muriel McKay never was discovered. Exactly how she died, where she died and when she died remains unsolved. The considerable efforts of the police to elicit a full confession from the Hosein brothers proved – and still prove – futile.

The brothers were found guilty of the murder of Muriel McKay, even in the absence of her body. The massive weight of circumstantial evidence which the police collected against them was compounded by the matching of Arthur Hosein's fingerprints to those not only on the letters from the 'M3 gang' to the McKay family, but also on a copy of the *Sunday People* newspaper which, ironically, the brothers had dropped in the drive of the McKays' house when they staged the kidnap.

During three days of intensive interrogation at Kingston Police Station in Surrey, the true characters of the Hosein brothers emerged. Weak, easily-dominated Nizamodeen cracked quickly, and twice tried to take his own life. At one stage, when asked where he was on the night of 29 December 1969, he replied in a state of panic: 'Oh, my! What has Arthur done to me? Where did Arthur say I was? I was with my brother Arthur.' Later, he threw his arms around a detective's shoulders and sobbed: 'Kill me. What have I done? Arthur always gets me into trouble. Kill me now.' Nizamodeen's defence lawyers even found it difficult to communicate with him. In deep shock, he completely refused for six weeks even to discuss the murder case with them, until finally they persuaded him to study statements made by the prosecution witnesses.

In contrast, Arthur, while never confessing to the murder of Mrs McKay, put on a show of bravado. Described by one senior officer as 'an aggressive psychopath', he would sit in the interview room dictating statements at a ferocious pace. At one stage he boasted to his interrogator that he intended to write a book about the McKay case and turn it into a film, starring Richard Burton as the policeman in command and Sammy Davis Junior as himself. Arthur's bombast and apparent unconcern at the charge of murder he was facing astonished detectives.

Even during their trial at the Old Bailey eight months after their arrest, the brothers played out their completely contrasting roles. Nizamodeen, pale and trembling, could barely be heard giving evidence in the witness-box, even with a microphone strapped around his neck. Arthur, on the other hand, was full of himself as ever. Having convinced himself he would be acquitted – a belief he confided to cellmates and police alike – he launched into an astonishing diatribe when convicted by the jury, yelling at the judge, Mr Justice Sebag Shaw: 'Injustice has not only been done, it has also been seen and heard by the gallery to have been done. They have seen the provocation of your lordship and they have seen your immense partiality.' Unmoved, the judge passed life sentences on both brothers, with further 25-year and 15-year sentences of imprisonment on Arthur and Nizamodeen respectively for the other charges relating to Mrs McKay's abduction.

During the months between the Hoseins' arrest and their trial, the police continued their desperate, fruitless search for the body of Muriel McKay. One inmate who shared a cell with Arthur while on remand claimed that he had told him that the body was disposed of in a reservoir. Police drained the huge site Arthur had named but, again, to no avail. The story was dismissed as having been either another instance of Arthur's many fantasies or an attempt by his fellow prisoner to swap phoney evidence for some sort of remission deal.

Eventually the police were forced to abandon their search – leaving forever three vital, unanswered questions. They are still unsolved: how was she murdered, when was she murdered and where was she murdered? Was she, it is still suggested, the victim of an indescribable fate and fed to the pigs of Rooks Farm? Only two men know the answers: Arthur and Nizamodeen Hosein.

In a final, heart-rending postscript to one of Britain's most perplexing, unsolved cases, the *Sun* newspaper published a statement from Alick McKay the morning after the trial of the Hoseins ended. It said:

'One can accept death in the ordinary way. It is something which has to be faced and one has to adjust one's life to take account of it.

But in these circumstances, one is unable to accept the explanation of death without finding a body, although I am convinced Muriel is never coming home again. I must face this situation of course and face my life as best I can.

I suppose I do not want to know the brutal facts really, and yet I must always ask, how did she die, what happened to her, where is her body?

However much I try to escape the tragedy and hurt of it, I suppose I really would like to know the answers . . .'

Doctor Death

An 84-year-old retired doctor died in July 1983 in the genteel Sussex seaside resort of Eastbourne. His passing might have warranted no more than a paragraph in the local paper, but for one thing ... The doctor, John Bodkin Adams, was believed by many to be a man who literally got away with mass murder. And it was only upon his death that newspapers could safely produce their dossiers on the astonishing case, in which Adams was tried at the Old Bailey for the murder of one of his patients, Edith Morrell, a 72-year-old widow. If he had been convicted he would have been charged with further murders. Two other charges had been prepared and the Crown believed it had sufficient evidence to prosecute three other cases.

Early in the investigation one of the policemen involved, Scotland Yard Detective Chief Superintendent Charles Hewitt, believed Adams killed nine of his elderly patients. He later increased his estimate to 25, believing that Adams had probably 'eased' many others out of this world after influencing them to change their wills in his favour.

But none of this came to light at the Old Bailey. Adams was acquitted after a classic courtroom duel between the then Attorney-General, Sir Reginald Manningham-Buller QC, and a brilliant defence lawyer, Geoffrey Lawrence.

Lawrence disliked his client intensely but he fought tigerishly, turning the Attorney-General's over-confidence against him in a brilliant tactical coup which is still recalled and admired by lawyers. Manningham-Buller was certain he would destroy Adams once he had him in the witness-box. Lawrence simply told Adams to exercise his right to remain silent – and thus avoid cross-examination. It was that, the police and prosecution believed, that saved him from the rope. For with the linchpin of the Crown's case snatched away, the jury took just 45 minutes to find him not guilty.

The trial was such a disaster that the Director of Public Prosecutions lost confidence that a conviction on any other charge could be procured. So he announced there would be no further action.

What the jury never knew – and could not in law be told – was that the police had investigated the deaths of a further 400 of his patients. They had also exhumed the bodies of two of the women who had not been cremated. They had prepared cases on the deaths of nine patients and had evidence pointing to the murder of many others.

The police knew that over his 35 years of practice in Eastbourne, Adams had been the beneficiary of 132 wills, amassing £45,000 in cash – worth ten

Dr John Bodkin Adams

times that today – antique silver, jewellery, furniture and cars, including two Rolls-Royces, from the bequests of dead patients.

So was John Bodkin Adams merely a plausible rogue or was he the most cunning mass murderer of the century?

He was certainly the most fashionable doctor in Eastbourne, a town where the elderly could spend their last days peacefully in genteel retirement. He had arrived there virtually straight from medical school in his native Northern Ireland and built up a good practice with the cream of the town as his patients.

He was an ugly man, only 1.7 m (5 ft 5 in) tall and weighing almost 114 kg (18 stone), with a pink fleshy face, small eyes and thin lips and a rolling chin that sagged over the celluloid collars he wore. But to his elderly women patients he was charming. He caressed their hands and combed their hair.

However, the picture painted by the year-long investigation by Mr Hewitt, then a sergeant, and his 'governor' Detective Chief Superintendent Bert Hannam of the Yard's Murder Squad, was this:

Adams made his victims dependent on his drugs. They craved his morphine and heroin and became addicts. He influenced them to change their wills in his favour. Then they died.

His method, the police claimed, was not startling, shocking or gory. He eased them gently out of life with an overdose of drugs.

Scotland Yard's investigations showed that of all the patients for whom Adams signed death certificates, he explained an improbable 68 per cent as being due to either cerebral haemorrhage or cerebral thrombosis.

Even before the war there was gossip that Adams did his rounds with a bottle of morphia in one pocket and a blank form in the other. In 1936 he had been the beneficiary in the will of Mrs Alice Whitton, to the extent of £3,000 – a substantial amount then. Her niece contested the will in the High Court but Adams won and kept the money.

The tongues continued to wag into the mid-1950s. But it was not until 1956 that police investigations actually began and the evidence started to build, much of it circumstantial.

There was the case of William Mawhood, a wealthy steel merchant, who was such a long-standing friend of Adams that he lent him £3,000 to buy his first house. As Mawhood lay dying, Adams asked his wife Edith to leave the bedside for a moment. She heard Adams say: 'Leave your estate to me and I'll look after your wife.'

Mrs Mawhood rushed back into the bedroom. She said later:

> 'I grabbed my gold-headed walking stick and struck out at the doctor and chased him around the bed. He ran out of the room and as he dashed down the stairs I threw my stick at him. Unfortunately

it missed, and broke a flower vase. I shouted to him to get out of the house. It was the last I wanted to see of him. I certainly would not tolerate the idea of Adams trying to get into my husband's will.'

There was the case of Emily Mortimer, whose family had a strict tradition, designed to keep its fortune intact. Whenever a Mortimer died, the bulk of the estate was divided among the surviving members of the family.

Adams persuaded Emily to break the tradition. In the year she died, she added a codicil to her will, transferring £3,000 worth of shares from the family to the doctor. Shortly before her death, she changed the will again so that Adams received £5,000 and members of the family were cut out. Adams signed the death certificate – the cause of death 'Cerebral thrombosis'.

Police discovered the case of the two old women who were persuaded by Adams to let him sell their house and move into a flat for the good of their health. He then refused to hand over the money from the house sale until forced to do so by a writ two years later.

Statements from local solicitors and bank managers on the doctor's insistent concern with the wills of his patients revealed a host of questionable activities. Visits to banks with patients to change details of wills already made; telephone calls to solicitors insisting on their immediate attendance to change or draw up a new will; a comatose patient who signed his altered will only with an X; wills changed on several occasions so that the deceased were cremated instead of buried as originally stipulated; and 32 cheques for the doctor amounting to £18,000 drawn on one old lady's account in the last few days of her life – and with highly suspect signatures.

Odious as such unprofessional behaviour was, it was not evidence of intent to murder. There was, however, plenty of other evidence ...

Clara Neil-Miller was an elderly spinster who had lived in genteel retirement with her sister Hilda for 13 years. When Hilda died she left everything to Clara. When Clara died, 13 months later, she bequeathed the bulk of her estate – £5,000 – to Adams.

Three years later the police exhumed both bodies and the post-mortem showed that Clara had died of pneumonia, not coronary thrombosis as Adams had put on the death certificate. Then one of the other guests in the rest home for the elderly where she died told the police:

'Dr Adams was called to Miss Clara the night before she died. She was suffering from influenza. He remained in her bedroom for nearly 45 minutes before leaving. I later became worried as I heard nothing from the room. I opened the door and was horrified by what I saw.

This was a bitterly cold winter's night. The bedclothes on her bed had been pulled back and thrown over the bedrail at the base. Her nightdress had been folded back across her body to her neck. All the bedroom windows had been flung open. A cold gush of wind was sweeping through the room. That is how the doctor had left her.'

Police found that, in addition to the £5,000 bequest, Clara had, in the weeks before her death, made out cheques for £300 and £500 to the doctor. The purpose was not clear. It could not be for medical treatment as, apart from the flu, she was not ill. Nor did she receive much in the way of medicines.

Adams had a financial interest in the rest home and sent many patients there. A potential key witness was the woman who ran it, Mrs Elizabeth Sharp. Ex Detective Chief Superintendent Hewitt recalled:

'Mrs Sharp was on the point of talking when we left Eastbourne for a week's conferences with the Attorney-General in London. She was the witness we needed. She knew much of what went on between Adams and his patients. She knew where the bodies were buried and she was scared and frightened. When we left, she was about to crack.

One more visit was all we needed, but when we were in London she died. When we got back to Eastbourne and heard the news, she had already been cremated on the doctor's instructions.

I always had a feeling, but no positive clue, that Adams speeded her on the way. It was too much of a coincidence when she died.'

Then there was the case of Julia Bradnum, a strong and healthy 82-year-old until one morning when she woke up with stomach pains. The doctor was called and remained in the room with her for five minutes. Ten minutes later she was dead.

Her body was also exhumed but it was too decomposed to show much more than that she had not died of the cerebral haemorrhage Adams' certificate claimed.

Only a few weeks before she died Adams had brought her a new will. He said something about her other will not being legal, she later told a friend, Miss Mary Hine. 'She asked me if I would witness the new one,' Miss Hine said. 'Dr Adams pointed to a spot on the paper where I was to sign. I turned over the paper to see what I was witnessing, but Dr Adams put his hand on the writing and turned it back.'

Another of the doctor's patients was Harriet Maud Hughes, aged 66, whom Adams had started to treat only three months before her death of 'cerebral thrombosis'. She spoke of changing her will in his favour. A few weeks before her death, she became ill but then recovered sufficiently to go to her bank with the doctor, who asked the bank manager in her presence to make him the executor of her will. Afterwards, she told her domestic help:

'You should have seen the bank manager's face. He was most surprised at my choice of executor.'

After her death it was discovered that she had added two codicils to her will. The first that she should be cremated. The second, added a month later, left £1,000 each to a Mr and Mrs Thurston, acquaintances of Dr Adams. After the death, the police discovered Adams received 90 per cent of the bequests – giving the Thurstons 10 per cent for the use of their name.

Then there was the case of James Priestly Downs, a wealthy retired bank manager and widower who in his last days tried nine times to sign his will while in a drugged state. On the tenth occasion he signed it with an X. Adams guided his hand. The will left the doctor £1,000. All Mr Downs was being treated for was a fractured ankle. After a fortnight of the treatment, however, he was in a coma. A month later he died.

Annabelle Kilgour was a widow who had been ill for several weeks and was being looked after by a State Registered Nurse, Miss Osgood. One night Adams arrived and said he would give an injection to help her get a good night's sleep.

The nurse was astounded as she watched the doctor give what she regarded as being greatly in excess of the normal dose. 'This will keep her quiet,' he said, and left.

It did. She immediately fell into a coma and died the next morning. When Adams arrived, the nurse told him: 'Mrs Kilgour is dead. You realize, doctor, that you have killed her?'

The nurse later told the Yard men: 'I have never seen a man look so frightened in all my life.'

Once again Adams gave the cause of death as cerebral haemorrhage. In her will, Mrs Kilgour left the doctor a sum of money and an antique clock.

Margaret Pilling, a member of one of Lancashire's richest cotton families, was suffering from nothing more serious than flu when Adams was called to her. Within a fortnight she was practically in a coma. But her family insisted she should go to stay with them.

Her daughter, Mrs Irene Richardson, said later:

'At first we thought she was dying of cancer and that the doctor was being kind by not telling us. But we held a family conference and decided we were not satisfied with the treatment. Whatever her illness, she was definitely being drugged. Her condition was deteriorating rapidly.'

We took a house for her at Ascot, near one of her relatives. Within a fortnight she was on her feet and at the races. Had I not taken her away, I am quite satisfied she would have died.

But the case that really clinched the matter, as far as the police were concerned, was when Bobbie Hullett, a friend of the Chief Constable Richard Walker, died. Mrs Hullett, a vivacious woman of 49 widowed four months earlier, was not even really ill.

Late in 1955 her husband Jack, a retired Lloyds underwriter, became ill. 'Thank God I have a good doctor,' he told one of his nurses. When he was stricken by a heart condition one night in March the next year, the 'good doctor' sat on his bed and injected a dose of morphia. Seven hours later Jack Hullett died. In his will he left Adams £500. The residue went to Bobbie, who was shocked and grief-stricken. Friends rallied round – none more so than Adams, who prescribed drugs to help her sleep. In four months she was dead.

Perhaps in the beginning the sleeping drugs were a wise practice. But as the weeks passed the dosage was not cut down. The domestic staff said later: 'She staggered downstairs most mornings as though she was drunk.'

One of her closest friends was comedian Leslie Henson. He said: 'Her death shocked me greatly. My wife and I saw her turning into a drug addict. We invited her to our home to get away from everything, but she rushed back after 24 hours to get to her pills again. We saw her disintegrating mentally through them.'

After her death another of her friends, Chief Constable Walker, began to make a few discreet phone calls. It was established that two days before Bobbie fell into the coma from which she never recovered, she gave Adams a cheque for £1,000. He immediately drove to the bank and asked for a special clearance. Within hours the amount was credited to his account. At the time, Dr Adams' bank accounts had £35,000 in them. With his investment holdings amounting to a further £125,000, he was not exactly in urgent need of money.

At the inquest, Adams was severely criticized by the coroner for his diagnosis and treatment. A number of penetrating questions were asked. Why had he not told his co-doctor, called in as a second opinion, of his patient's depressive medical history? Why had he failed to get proper daytime medical attention for her or had her put in a nursing home? Why, after 34 years as a doctor, did he take the advice of a young house surgeon in administering a new drug? Why had he failed to call in a psychiatric consultant? And why had he persisted in his diagnosis of a cerebral catastrophe after a pathologist had suggested it might be poisoning?

The doctor replied: 'I honestly did what I thought was best for her.'

The coroner was unimpressed. 'There has been an extraordinary degree of careless treatment,' he said.

And that was the moment that Chief Constable Walker called in Scotland Yard.

So what went wrong? Why, in the face of all this evidence, was John

Bodkin Adams not charged with other offences? Why did the prosecution choose to concentrate on the case of Edith Morrell, the 72-year-old widow of a wealthy Liverpool shipping merchant?

One prosecution lawyer said afterwards: 'We chose it because it was such a clear and obvious case of murder that I should have thought no jury could have regarded it in any other way.'

But Mr Hewitt says:

'Adams was allowed to escape because the law made an ass of itself. I will never forget that conference we had with Manningham-Buller in the Attorney-General's office at the House of Commons. Bert Hannam and I felt sick with disbelief when he announced he was going for Mrs Morrell. It was madness when we had so many better cases, with more specific evidence – and, what's more important, with bodies.

Mrs Morrell had been cremated. This meant we could not use evidence of the best forensic scientist of the day, Dr Francis Camps. But Manningham-Buller was so arrogant he would not listen to his junior counsel, Melford Stevenson and Malcolm Morris, or Mr Leck of the Director of Public Prosecutions' office.

He knew the doctor was a worried man and he would destroy him in the witness-box. But it never happened because Manningham-Buller never considered for a moment that Adams might not be called to give evidence.'

Adams came to trial on 25 April 1957 – six years after Mrs Morrell's death. Prosecution witnesses testified that over a period of six weeks, Adams had prescribed a massive dose of more than 4,000 grains of barbiturate and heroin for Mrs Morrell.

The British Pharmaceutical Association's recommended maximum daily dosage was a quarter morphia grain. But in the last day of her life Adams injected into his barely conscious patient 18 grains of the drug, they said.

But Geoffrey Lawrence managed to discover the nurses' daily record books which gave a more accurate account of the medicine Adams prescribed than the memories of the nurses themselves. Then came his master stroke of not putting Adams into the box.

Three months after his acquittal Adams appeared at Lewes Assizes and pleaded guilty to 14 charges, including the forgery of National Health Service prescriptions and failing to keep a record of dangerous drugs. He was fined £2,400 and ordered to pay costs. In November that year he was struck off by the General Medical Council.

On 22 November 1961, at the age of 62, he was readmitted to the medical register, an event which went largely unnoticed. Only the Home Office retained some doubts: his licence to dispense dangerous drugs was never returned.

His practice in Eastbourne picked up again, although never to its previous size. In 1965, a grateful patient left £2,000 to Adams in her will.

Shortly before his death Adams was interviewed at his Eastbourne home. He refused to talk about his personal life. 'I don't want any more publicity,' he said. 'I have had too much of it. God knows, I have.'

The Nazis' Gold

War is the ideal cover for crime. World war provides an even more effective diversion. While the Nazi war machine fanned across Europe in World War 2, a criminal operation was carried out on the most colossal scale . . .

Quite simply, Adolf Hitler and his generals set about systematically stealing the untold wealth of conquered countries in an orgy of blatant crime-for-profit. Like 20th-century pirates, they planned to make themselves rich in plunder at the expense of their victims. They stole not only the few miserable possessions of the millions of Jews they sent to the death camps. They literally stripped sovereign nations of their entire wealth – billions and billions of pounds in gold and diamonds and works of art. From the treasure houses of the former Czars, deep inside Russia, to the art galleries of Paris and the bank vaults of Rome, the Nazis stole and stole and stole.

Even decades after the end of the war, many governments still refuse to admit the extent of the fortunes stolen from them by the Nazis. Intelligence experts on both sides on the Iron Curtain estimate that as much as £50 billion worth of gold is still unaccounted for and that hundreds of Nazi crooks and their families are leading lives of luxury on the proceeds of the biggest robbery in history.

Much of the missing billions is still probably hidden inside Germany, sunk out of reach at the bottom of lakes or in the depths of collapsed mine shafts. Fortunes in gold were certainly channelled through Swiss bank accounts into the coffers of South American governments who charged £5 million a head to give sanctuary to fleeing Nazi criminals at the end of the war. But stunned and sickened by the debris of the war, grimly completing the task of counting the toll in death and destruction, the Allied forces gave a low priority to tracking down stolen cash and bullion. By the time they started trying to recover the astronomical sums of wealth stolen by the Nazis, the fortune had vanished into the creaking remains of the international banking system. Stolen Nazi gold is undoubtedly the basis for many of the multi-national businesses which flourish today.

In their panic-stricken flight, however, many Nazis found the sheer bulk of their loot impossible to move and they literally dumped billions by the roadsides of Europe. Even now those caches of casually hidden treasure are being uncovered. In June 1983 workmen renovating the well of an abandoned monastery in northern Italy, near the Austrian border, found the shaft blocked by heavy metal chests. They finally raised them, and counted 60 tons of gold, worth more than £540 million at 1983 prices.

An embarrassed Italian government then admitted publicly for the first time that the Nazis, their wartime Allies, had emptied the Central Bank of Rome in 1944 and had made off with 120 tons of gold. The scramble to prove ownership of the gold brought a counter-claim from neighbouring Yugoslavia that the bullion was just part of the reserves from their own national bank in Zagreb, looted by Nazi occupying forces and loaded into a convoy of trucks to be driven back to the Fatherland.

Throughout the history of warfare, victorious soldiers have plundered and looted their vanquished opponents. The looters have ranged from humble infantrymen who 'liberated' enemy wine cellars to high-ranking officers who commandeered whole castles for their private estates. Their motto: To the victor belong the spoils.

For Adolf Hitler's Third Reich, however, there was to be no petty thieving. With Teutonic thoroughness, the thefts were to be carried out on a grand scale, meticulously planned and on the direct orders of the Führer himself. Organized bank robbery was as much a declared war policy of the Nazis as the conquest of Europe and the mass murder of the Jews. The formation of an official looting department in the Nazi government was born out of Hitler's smouldering resentment of his fellows.

As a brooding teenager, Adolf Hitler moved to the Austrian town of Linz in 1903, after the death of his father in their home town of Braunau, some 20 miles away. He struggled through school, ignored by teachers and disliked by his fellow pupils, nursing only an ambition to become an artist. When his mother died in 1908, Hitler, then 19 years old, felt free to leave Linz and take his meagre talents to the glittering Austrian capital of Vienna. He marvelled at the city's splendid galleries and museums and his first call was on the Academy of Fine Arts where he applied for enrolment as a student. The

Priceless treasure is unearthed at Hermann Goering's castle

Academy examiners were unimpressed with his barely competent portfolio of drawings and recommended he try for training elsewhere, perhaps in the less demanding profession of apprentice draughtsman.

For the next few years, until he left for Munich in 1913, Hitler seethed with anger as he scraped a miserable living in doss-houses, selling his poorly painted watercolours to bar-room patrons who pitied him because he looked so ragged and pathetic. The experience left him with a sense of humiliation which remained with him for more than 20 years, until he became the all-powerful Führer and annexed Austria into the Greater Germany. That is when Hitler became master of Vienna – and had his revenge on the city he despised.

As he planned to launch war on the rest of Europe, so Hitler also planned his artistic revenge on the cultured city of Vienna. In March 1938, while

Recaptured treasure is inspected at New York's United Nations Galleries

basking in a rapturous welcome from the citizens of the drab town of Linz, his adopted home, he summoned the director of the town's provincial museum, Dr Karl Kerschner. 'I will make Linz the art capital of the world,' he promised him. 'It will have the finest treasures all of Europe can provide. I will make those ungrateful peasants of Vienna feel they are living in a slum.'

Then Hitler, the failed artist, began to sketch out his amateur architectural plans for rebuilding the city, centred around his dream of a Führermuseum which would be crammed with paintings and sculpture, tapestries and rare books, and all the golden treasures he could loot from the four corners of Europe. He sent for his squat, bloodthirsty deputy, Martin Bormann, and instructed him: 'Wherever German tanks roll, I want them to bring back to Linz all the treasures they can carry.'

And so was formed Sonderauftrag Linz – the Linz Special Mission – history's only example of a select gang of gold bullion robbers, diamond, jewel and art thieves, armed with bombers, tanks, high explosives and carte blanche to murder on behalf of their Government. But before the looting gangs bothered to turn their attentions to the treasure houses beyond Germany's boundaries, they first set out ruthlessly stripping the fortunes of their own tortured Jewish population.

While Hitler ordered vaults to be built inside the air-raid shelters of Munich as temporary store-rooms for the Linz collection, his special squad began to 'confiscate' the belongings of Jewish families. Their first target was Baron Louis von Rothschild, the richest man in Austria. Rothschild was arrested by the Gestapo and interrogated by Hitler's roving art and bullion assessor, Dr Hans Posse of the Dresden Art Museum.

Baron Louis was stripped of all his possessions, as a colossal ransom to allow him and his family to leave the country and escape from Nazi persecution. His priceless collection of gold coins was seized, together with all his valuable works of art including paintings by Van Dyck, Holbein, Tintoretto and Gainsborough.

Fortunes fell into Nazi hands even before their armies began to cross the borders into the Netherlands, Belgium and France. As fear and panic spread through the wealthy and well-to-do classes of Europe, Jews and non-Jews alike, homes and possessions were sold at give-away prices and the dwindling assets of great merchant families began pouring into the banks of neutral Switzerland.

Martin Bormann was one of the Nazi hierarchy given the task of trying to harass and bully the Swiss bankers into handing over the accounts of clients whose funds had been earmarked for seizure by the German government. Scornfully oblivious to the wrath of the Nazis, the bank managers of Geneva and Basle stood firm. They would not even discuss the identities of their clients. Ironically, a few years later, that lesson was not to be lost on the Nazi leaders who had cursed the tight-lipped Swiss money men.

As Hitler's war machine rumbled through Europe, with the Führer's hand-picked vultures following in their tracks, the section leaders of Sonderauftrag Linz were swamped. They could no longer cope with the tidal wave of treasure which began piling up in the Munich air-raid shelters. They were furiously building new offices to house the records of their glittering hoard when the most glittering prize of all fell into their hands – Paris.

Enough gold and works of art had already been allocated to the Linz project to transform the town many times over. And now the untold wealth of the Louvre, the Palace of Versailles and the vaults of the Bank of France were at their mercy. Even veteran looter Hans Posse was overwhelmed. So another unit was established specially to supervise the pillage of Paris. Art expert Alfred Rosenberg was given his own top priority organization to strip France of its national heritage and to transport the country's wealth back to Germany.

Rosenberg, son of an Estonian shoemaker, set about his task with gusto, hampered only by the overwhelming greed of the obese Luftwaffe chief Hermann Goering. The air marshal could not resist setting out to build up his own personal fortune, diverting train loads of looted art works and gold to his own private estate, Karinhall, near Berlin.

For four years the Nazi leaders stole everything they could lay their hands on. From Russia came the treasure of the palaces of Emperor Alexander and Empress Catherine. While German infantrymen died of starvation and exposure trying to capture the cities of Stalingrad and Leningrad, the looting sections plundered a total of 427 museums and banks, transporting their booty back to Berlin in fifty special trains each month.

The bank vaults of Poland and Czechoslovakia were stripped and two thirds of the national wealth of Belgium and Holland were stolen. By 1944 it was estimated that the Nazis had plundered a staggering total of £15 billion from occupied countries, worth about twenty times that amount at present-day prices. Goering's own personal fortune was built on his share of 21,903 objects of art shipped back from France.

Then the tide of war turned against the Nazis.

Hitler's dream of his Imperial Museum at Linz began to crumble as Allied bombers hit deeper and deeper into the heart of Germany. With defeat staring them in the face, the Nazis scrambled to dispose of their loot. The salt mines of the remote Austrian village of Alt Ausee were crammed with art treasures and gold, the Hohenfurth monastery, just inside the Czech border, was filled with diamonds and the castle of Schloss Neuschwanstein, near Fussen, Bavaria, packed with bullion. For the demented Führer there was no

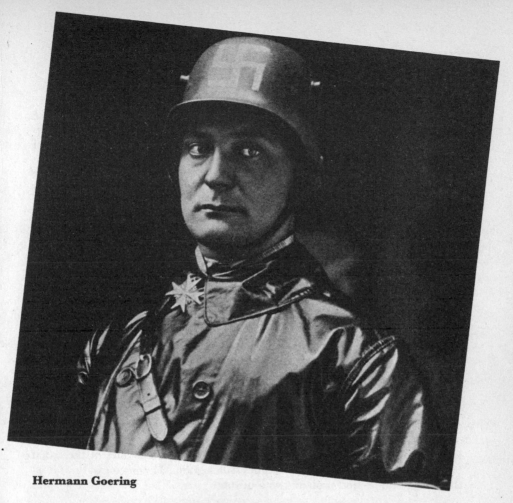

Hermann Goering

hiding place where he could scuttle for safety. But those of his accomplices who thought they could save their own skins met in Berlin to form the secret organization Odessa, devoted to financing the escape of the most wanted men in Europe. At their disposal were billions of pounds. War criminals like Bormann, death camp doctor Joseph Mengele and extermination leaders Adolf Eichmann and Walter Rauff began to bless the secrecy of Swiss banks. Using the same well-oiled banking system which had helped to protect some of their victims a few years earlier, the Odessa men funnelled gold through secret accounts to buy themselves new identities and safety in South America. Vast ranches and villas throughout Argentina, Bolivia, Paraguay and Chile were established on the stolen wealth of the men who were never caught, whose crimes are still unpunished. Odessa spent recklessly to finance its fugitives, but it is certain that pockets of Nazi gold still lie undiscovered throughout Europe.

In 1982 Danish naval divers trying to locate sunken Nazi gold in Lake Ornso, in central Jutland, came under sniper fire. The theory police came up with at the time was that it was from a former Gestapo informer who feared the hoard might reveal details of his collaboration in looting Danish banks.

During the final collapse of Germany in May 1945, the most bizarre bank robbery in history took place as American and Russian troops raced each other into the heart of Berlin. The Americans were ordered by General Eisenhower to storm the Reichsbank in Berlin, blow the vaults and transport the contents by jeep and truck back behind American lines for safekeeping. The troops responded enthusiastically, but some £200 million in gold and negotiable Swiss securities went missing on the journey back to American headquarters. Three and a half decades later, in April 1979, three men in Ontario, Canada, were jailed for trading in some of those missing war-time securities. It is also estimated that American soldiers and stragglers from the German Army helped themselves to £90 million in gold bullion, foreign exchange and jewels from the bank. Not a penny was ever recovered and not a single soldier charged with robbery.

But South America was not the only final resting place for missing Nazi gold. In the United States and Europe the fortunes of respectable business empires thrive today on the proceeds of the Nazi looting during World War 2. Yet the wartime Allies have decided that the scandalous details of history's most massive unsolved robberies will never be published. At the headquarters of the British secret service and the World War 2 Records Division of the National Archives in Washington, the files holding the names of the worst criminals and the details of their crimes will remain Most Secret until at least the 21st century – and probably well beyond.

The Unpaid Debt

They called him Mr Big – the playboy gambler who could fix anything from a roulette wheel or stud poker game to the World Series baseball tournament. He lived a life of luxury and thought nothing of betting $4,000 on odd or even car number plates passing his hotel-room window. He won and lost fortunes on horses and cards; he bought and sold cops, politicians and financiers and was rarely seen without a beautiful showgirl on his arm.

Even on the day he was gunned down – 4 November 1928 – he was trying to talk his way out of an $80,000 gambling debt. But that debt, the one thing Arnold Rothstein could not fix, led to his shooting outside Park Central Hotel, New York.

Police were certain Rothstein knew his killer. Only half an hour before the shooting he took a telephone call in a Broadway restaurant. As he left, he told the head waiter: 'George McManus wants me.' Yet Rothstein died in hospital two days later, from a bullet wound in the stomach, without naming his killer. The only thing he did on his deathbed was to make a will – providing generously for his wife Carolyn, for Ziegfeld Follies showgirl Inez Norton (she got more than $100,000) and for friends.

Perhaps the oddest aspect was that the police had plenty of clues – an overcoat, four glasses and a revolver – yet they failed completely to get a conviction. The owner of the overcoat was another gambler, George McManus. The glasses and revolver were covered in fingerprints, some of them almost certainly those of known hoodlums. Only McManus was charged with the murder. He pleaded not guilty and was acquitted because of insufficient evidence. That was the end of the police investigation. Nobody else was charged and the case went on the 'unsolved' files.

There was talk at the time that McManus and his henchmen had 'nobbled' the cops. The then police commissioner was soon swept out of office. It is also possible that the police may have taken the view that since Rothstein was part of the underworld, his killer had done society a service . . .

In his 46 years Rothstein had become the 'King of the Gamblers'. He hobnobbed with gangsters such as Al Capone, Dion O'Bannion and Big Jim Colosimo and wagered around $10,000,000 on games of chance. He once backed Jack Dempsey to beat Jess Willard in a world heavyweight fight and won $200,000. He picked up $300,000 when he backed Gene Tunney against Dempsey. And in what he described as the 'biggest gamble of my life' he won almost $300,000 when a horse called Sidereal won at the Aqueduct track, Long Island, on Independence Day, 1921, at odds of 30-1.

Poker was another of his passions – and it was this that was to cost him his life. He sat in on a stud poker game with George McManus and other gamblers including 'Titanic' Thompson, so-called because of his reputation for 'sinking' opponents. At the end of two days and nights Rothstein owed $150,000. His biggest creditor, Nathan Raymond, to whom he owed $80,000, was in no mood to wait for his money. Rothstein had never welshed on a bet in his life. But this poker debt was to prove the exception. One underworld theory was that Rothstein had suspected he had been cheated, though he never made any accusation. It would certainly explain his reluctance to settle up – for he had assets to cover the debt many times over.

Over the next few weeks the gangster-gamblers put the squeeze on. But still Rothstein refused to pay up. Then on that fateful Sunday night in November, Rothstein went to Room 439 at Park Central Hotel to make his excuses to McManus.

The theory is that there was a lot of whiskey drunk and a lot of shouting – then McManus or one of his henchmen pulled a gun. Rothstein tried to wrest the gun from his killer, but in the struggle it went off and Rothstein fell to the floor. McManus and his gang fled, throwing the gun out of the window. Somehow Rothstein then staggered down two flights of stairs to the street. Police believe that Rothstein was murdered in the heat of the moment. Only one shot was fired – and gangsters intent on murder, they reasoned, usually pumped their victims full of lead.

But they are just theories. And George McManus, the one man who could have proved or disproved them, died in New Jersey in 1940 of natural causes.

The Black Widow

For a woman who did very little farming, widow Belle Gunness ate very well. While her neighbours in La Porte, Indiana, raised crops, Belle planted bodies and produced a bumper yield of dollars.

Once she had been Mads Sorenson's wife – but thanks to a stein of beer she gave him in their home on Lake Michigan, their marriage did not last long. The beer was generously laced with strychnine, and the self-made widow had Mads cremated before the insurance investigators knew what was happening. The company objected, but the policy brought her $8,500.

She had no trouble finding a new husband. At 31, Belle was still an attractive woman. It was an attraction that was to prove fatal for real estate promoter Peter Gunness of La Porte. Belle married Gunness and had three children – two girls and a boy –and a domestic life with which she was satisfied till the day the money ran out.

One day in December 1902, Gunness told Belle he was down to his final asset: a $10,000 insurance policy that would have to be cashed. He had invested everything in real estate options near a railroad that had never been built. Belle helped him find the policy and went with him to the door. As he turned to kiss her goodbye, she raised a meat cleaver and smashed it into his skull.

Gullible police accepted her story that Gunness had slipped on the icy pathway and had split his own skull against the doorstep. But the insurance underwriters were more suspicious and there was an investigation that lasted for months before Belle could cash her second husband's cheque.

Belle then began to publish advertisements in the lonely hearts columns of a Minneapolis newspaper. The bait was her sumptuous 12-room house on a 75-acre farm 'adjoining a boulevard'. And even more tempting to greedy or lonely men were her personal charms. She picked through the replies with care. She wanted men without relatives – but with plenty of cash.

George Berry of Tusca, Illinois, came first, in July 1905. He had obediently brought his life savings, $1,500 in cash. But he was puzzled by the sight of Belle, who had now become fat, walked with a waddle and had a growth of hair on her lip. She decoyed him from the station to her farmhouse with assurances that she was only the beautiful widow's maid. And while he waited patiently for the beauty to appear, she approached him through a side door with a well-honed axe in hand.

In the next year the farm had three other visitors all with their nest-eggs in hand. None were to leave.

In 1908 the black widow's pit claimed two more bodies. One was Andrew Helgelien, who wrote to Belle from Aberdeen, South Dakota – but chose to conceal the fact that he had an older brother named Asle.

When Asle heard nothing from his brother for two weeks, he sent a pointed letter of inquiry to Mrs Gunness. The widow replied that her Andy had mysteriously disappeared and begged Asle to come to La Porte and join her in the quest, bringing with him all the money he could raise. But the man who arrived was not Asle at all, it was the sheriff of La Porte county, tipped off by the suspicious brother. The widow pleaded for time. She had just heard from Andy, she told the sheriff, and would be able to produce the missing man if he came again the following day.

But the sheriff had to return to the murder farm before the end of the day. He was greeted by a curtain of red flame against the sky. It was the Guinness farmhouse, its old timbers reduced to charcoal in a matter of minutes. Under freshly turned earth at the back of the barn, the sheriff found six corpses. The first was that of Andrew Helgelien. In the ashes of the house were four more bodies – three of them small, one large. Belle and her children?

The authorities wanted to believe so, but there was macabre evidence which meant they could never close the file on Belle Gunness. A witness said that an hour before the fire he had seen the widow drive past his farm with a wagon and a team of horses. And in one of the local cemeteries next day, there were reports of mysterious vandalism – the gravestones of an adult and three children had been dislodged.

Unrelenting to the end of his life, Asle Helgelien went on looking for the widow. He never found her.

The Wreck of the Chantiloupe

When winter storms lash the sea to boiling and great waves pound across the bay, villagers snug in their cottages shudder at the memory of a hideous crime that taints them still. There are those who swear that, above the roar of the wind and breakers crashing on the shore, they have heard the screams of men and women who perished in a shipwreck more than 200 years ago.

But not all those who died were victims of the cruel elements. At least one, a wealthy woman passenger, was killed for her jewellery by heartless looters. Their names have remained a shameful secret ever since.

In summer, Thurlestone Sands, in south Devon, ring with the happy laughter of romping children, and the sunbathers soak up the warmth. But in winter, long after the last holidaymaker has gone home, as the gales howl in from the Atlantic, it is easy to picture the last moments of the Plymouth-bound brig *Chantiloupe* in 1772.

It had been a smooth voyage from the West Indies but, as she neared port, a south-westerly gale blew up so suddenly that there was no time to turn into it. The captain's only choice was to run before it, past Plymouth and up the Channel. Soon, with massive cliffs looming ahead, he was forced to strike sail and drop all anchors. But nothing could hold the *Chantiloupe* against the raging wind and sea, and the captain decided on a desperate gamble to save his passengers and crew.

Ordering full sail, he altered course by a few degrees and headed directly for the smooth, golden carpet of Thurlestone Sands. He told passengers and crew that he aimed to run his ship high up the beach, so they could all jump to safety.

The passengers hurried to their cabins to collect what valuables they could. One of them, Mrs James Burke, whose nephew was the famous Whig politician Edmund Burke, came on deck in her finest gown wearing all her jewellery.

The small ship raced for the shore as though on wings, carried on the shoulders of mighty waves, and it seemed the captain's daring bid would succeed. But one wave, higher than the rest, suddenly hoisted the stern. The keel beneath the bows struck bottom and the *Chantiloupe* swung broadside, almost capsizing under the next wave.

All on board were hurled into the raging sea, and most died within minutes. But Mrs Burke struck out for the shore and, miraculously, reached it alive. Gratefully she let strong hands grasp her and pull her from the water.

But these three men were not rescuers ... they were thieves and killers. Barely had her last scream been carried away by the wind before they were fighting over her jewels.

They ripped off her earrings and, finding her rings too tight to remove, hacked off her fingers. Then they buried her in the sand, and soon the raging sea had washed away any traces of the killing.

Perhaps it would never have come to light, if a man had not happened to walk his dog past the burial spot two weeks later. He was Daniel Whiddon, later to be immortalized in the folk song 'Uncle Tom Cobleigh'. His dog began scrabbling in the sand and unearthed Mrs Burke's body.

The secret was out, and the local paper reported the crime in these words:
'The savage people from the adjacent villages, who were
anxiously waiting for the wreck, seized and stript her of her clothes,
even cutting off some of her fingers and mangling her ears in their
impatience to secure the jewels and left her miserable to perish.'

There was an autopsy, which showed that Mrs Burke was alive when she reached the shore. An inquest, before the jury of local men, returned the verdict: 'Murder by person or persons unknown.'

There can be no doubt that some people in the nearby villages of Thurlestone Sands, Galmpton, Hope and Bolberry, knew the identity of the killers. But lips were sealed. Edmund Burke himself visited the area to seek the truth, and learned nothing.

More than 100 years later, the Rev Frank Coope, Rector of Thurlestone from 1897 to 1921, probed the mystery. He wrote: 'It was well known in the neighbourhood who did it, and their surnames are remembered to this day. The three men who were "in it" all came, it is said, to a bad end within the year. One hanged himself in an outhouse, another went mad, ran into the sea and was drowned, and the third was killed in an accident.'

Was this the truth – or a tale to put the rector off the scent?

Today the neatly thatched villages around Thurlestone Sands are picturesque and welcoming. But behind the whitewashed walls and stout oak doors, there may still be families who know the names of those long-ago killers.

Chapter
Four

Vanishing
Tricks

The Disappearing Parachutist

The skyjacker who commandeered the Northwest Airlines Boeing 727 flight from Portland, Oregon, to Seattle, Washington, was cold, calculating and ruthless. He terrified the cabin staff when he opened the canvas bag he was carrying in his lap and showed them a home-made bomb – tightly wrapped sticks of dynamite packed round a detonator.

As the jet cruised at 6,000 m (20,000 ft) above the Cascade Mountains, he threatened to blow apart the aircraft, killing himself and the 35 other passengers on board.

But the man who cruelly bargained with the lives of the passengers and the crew pulled off such a daring and lucrative coup that he is now fondly remembered as a folk hero, a swashbuckling pirate of the jet age. Songs have been written in his honour, fan clubs have been formed to cherish his memory and thousands of his admirers wear T-shirts emblazoned with his name. The souvenir industry and the posters in praise of D. B. Cooper would undoubtedly carry his photograph and glowing testimonials about his personal history – if anyone knew what he looked like or who he really was.

But the true identity of the man who literally vanished into thin air with his $200,000 booty still remains a mystery. No-one knows who he was, where he came from or where he went.

D. B. Cooper may be a frozen corpse, a broken body lying in a mouldering heap of banknotes in an impenetrable forest in the mountains of the northwestern United States. Or he may be sunning himself on a beach in Mexico and gloating over his perfect crime.

The last confirmed sighting of D. B. Cooper came from the pilot of the Boeing air liner from which the skyjacker leaped clutching a white cloth bag containing ten thousand $20 bank notes. Cooper vanished into thin air at 2,000 m (7,000 ft) as the air whistled past in a 90 metre per second (200 m.p.h) slipstream at a temperature of −23°C (−10°F).

That was the last time 'D. B. Cooper' was seen. The first time was in the departure lounge at Portland Airport, Oregon, when he bought his one-way ticket for the 400-mile journey to Seattle, Washington. It was 24 November 1971 – Thanksgiving Day – and the other travellers were all anxious to get home to their families for the annual holiday celebration.

The quiet middle-aged man with the canvas carrier bag and dark, tinted glasses paid cash for his ticket and gave his name as 'D. B. Cooper'. After a 45-minute wait in the lounge, where no one looked at him twice, he filed aboard when the flight was called and the jet roared off into the darkening skies.

Halfway through the one-hour flight, Cooper pushed the button in the overhead panel to summon one of the cabin crew to his seat. Stewardess Tina Mucklow approached with a tray, ready to take his order for a drink.

Cooper simply thrust a crumpled note into her hand and then reached under his seat to pull his canvas bag on to his lap. He waited a few seconds for the stewardess to read the note. It warned: 'I have a bomb with me. If I don't get $200,000 I will blow us all to bits.'

As the terrified stewardess tried to control her panic, Cooper calmly opened the bag to let her glimpse the dynamite and detonator inside. While the girl walked slowly up to the flight deck, Cooper settled back in his seat and peered out at the storm clouds below.

Within seconds a special transmitter on the flight deck of the Boeing was 'squawking' its coded electronic message over the radio frequencies ... 'Hijack ... Hijack ... Hijack ...'

At Seattle Airport a team of FBI agents, local police sharpshooters, hostage negotiation experts and airline officials were hastily gathered as the plane prepared to land. The passengers were still unaware of the drama when the jet came in for a perfect touchdown and rolled gently to a halt at the end of the runway.

There was a groan of annoyance from the impatient travellers when the captain made the terse announcement: 'Ladies and gentlemen, there will be a slight delay in disembarking. Please remain in your seats until we are ready to taxi to the terminal building.'

Only one passenger ignored the announcement. Cooper unbuckled his seat belt and, clutching his bag, walked swiftly up to the flight deck and positioned himself behind the crew. 'Now gentlemen,' he said softly, 'don't bother to look round.'

In 20 minutes of unyielding demands over the ground control radio from the flight deck of the airliner, Cooper stuck to his original threat and no one dared to call his bluff.

As the passengers began to grow more and more restless, there was a hiss of pneumatic power and the forward door of the Boeing slid open. The flight engineers in overalls – undercover armed FBI men – came aboard with a trolley of 'catering equipment'. They clearly saw the figure of the man with the canvas bag watching them from the flight deck door, then, under instructions by two-way radio from their superiors, they withdrew and the door slid closed and locked again.

The trolley was wheeled up to the flight deck by a stewardess and Cooper studied its contents. It contained a tough white sack with $200,000 and two backpack and two chestpack parachutes.

Cooper complained that he wanted the money in a rucksack which he could have strapped on to his body. But he quickly relented and told the pilot: 'You can let the passengers go now.'

Loudly complaining, the unsuspecting travellers filed off the aircraft to a waiting bus and Seattle ground control breathed a sigh of relief. But they were still left with the problem of Cooper in charge of the aircraft and its three-man crew as the jet was refuelled to maximum capacity by two giant tankers.

Minutes before the Boeing took off again, three military pursuit fighters and a small fleet of helicopters were scrambled from Seattle Airport and a nearby US Air Force base with orders to try to keep the jet in sight.

'We are heading for Mexico now,' Cooper told the pilot, Captain W. Bill Scott. But 10 minutes after take-off he issued new instructions.

As the aircraft climbed away from Seattle and headed south, Cooper insisted with calm precision: 'Fly with the flaps lowered 15 per cent and the landing gear down, keep the speed below 90 metres per second (2000 m.p.h), don't climb above 2,000 m (7,000 ft) and open the rear door.'

'We'll burn up too much fuel,' Captain Scott protested. 'We'll have to put down for some more fuel if we fly like that.'

'OK,' Cooper snapped. 'Stop for refuelling in Reno, Nevada. I'll give you further orders there. Now just fly south and keep the door locked behind you.'

The hijacker paused only briefly on the flight deck to retrieve his ransom note from the captain's tunic pocket. He was determined not to leave any clues behind, not even a sample of his handwriting.

The whole aircraft filled with a deafening roar as the pilot throttled back and lowered the rear door ramp into the slipstream.

When the flight recorder 'black box' was checked later, the sensitive instrument measured a tiny change in the aircraft's altitude, equivalent to the loss of a weight of 73 kg (160 lb) in the tail section. The time was 20.13 hours, 32 minutes after leaving Seattle. That's when D. B. Cooper leaped out.

Four hours later, as the Boeing lost height and glided gently towards the twinkling lights of the airport at Reno in the Nevada Desert, the co-pilot unlocked the flight deck door to warn Cooper that the tail ramp would have to be closed for landing.

The cabin was deserted. Cooper and the money had gone.

Two parachutes had been left behind. A backpack chute was intact but a chestpack was ripped to shreds. Cooper had probably torn it apart to make a harness to strap his sack of money to his body.

The danger of mid-air death and destruction had passed. And the hunt to find D. B. Cooper was on. FBI and Federal Aviation Agency officials who plotted the flight path of the hijacked Boeing quickly realized that Cooper had bailed out over some of the most densely wooded, inhospitable mountains in the American West, where the chances of survival for an inexperienced woodsman were pretty slim. He had plummeted to earth clad only in a lightweight lounge suit, a raincoat and with a pair of flimsy moccasin shoes on his feet. In the thin atmosphere of the high altitude, the parachute would only have slowed him to a bone-crushing 18 metres per second (40 m.p.h.) before he hit the mountain peaks which tower up to the same height as the Boeing had flown.

Only a super-fit expert could have hoped to escape alive. Police began detailed and intensive scrutiny of the only group of men who would have the nerve or experience to attempt that kind of death-defying descent – the 'smoke jumpers' of the Forestry Service fire-fighting teams. But they drew a blank. Cooper was not a 'smoke jumper' and the professional experts who are trained to parachute into the high forests with full radio communication and ground support facilities agreed to a man that Cooper's leap from a speeding jet in a rain storm was suicidal.

Aerial searches covering thousands of square miles of the states of Oregon, Washington and Nevada failed to show any trace of a parachute canopy.

Then, three weeks after the hijack, came the first enigmatic clue. A typewritten note, posted in Seattle and signed by D. B. Cooper, arrived at a Los Angeles newspaper. The writer revealed:

'I am no modern-day Robin Hood, unfortunately I have only 14 months to live. The hijacking was the fastest and most profitable way to gain a few last grains of peace of mind. I didn't rob Northwest because I thought it would be romantic or heroic or any of the other euphemisms that seem to attach themselves to situations of high risk.

I don't blame people for hating me for what I've done nor do I blame anybody for wanting me caught or punished – though this can never happen. I knew from the start I would not be caught. I've come and gone on several airline flights since and I'm not holed up in some obscure backwoods town. Neither am I a psychopath, I've never even received a speeding ticket.'

The note sparked off a new hunt for Cooper and as the list of potential suspects dwindled, hundreds of troops from the Fort Lewis Army base in Portland, Oregon, were ordered to comb the mountains searching for clues. They were backed up by spotter planes and even satellite surveillance photographs from orbiting spacecraft.

There was still no sign of Cooper.

But FBI agents were confident that if Cooper had survived the jump, he would be nailed as soon as he tried to spend a penny of the ransom money. The serial numbers of every one of the bank notes in his haul had been noted and all US banks and major money clearing houses abroad had been alerted to raise the alarm as soon as they began to trickle into circulation.

In the meantime the airlines took the costly precaution of ensuring that no one would imitate Cooper's hijack and high level parachute escape ever again. All Boeing 727s were recalled to the manufacturers and their tail door ramps sealed so they could never be opened in flight.

And as the widely publicised FBI manhunt began to lose steam, the mystery hijacker began to gather a cult following from a fascinated public. Graffiti slogans appeared on public buildings and airline advertising hoardings over the Pacific north west – 'D. B. Cooper, where are you?' Disc jockeys dedicated records to Cooper.

A year after the hijack, when FBI officals adopted the official attitude that D. B. Cooper must have died in the parachute fall, they had to admit that there was no sign of the hijack money and that the $200,000 was probably still hidden with his body in the wooded mountains. Then the first groups of enthusiastic amateur explorers, calling themselves the 'Ransom Rangers', began scouring the woods in Oregon and Washington, searching for the ransom treasure.

Finally on 24 November 1976, the FBI officially closed the file on D. B. Cooper. Five years had elapsed since the crime, so under the Statute of Limitations if D. B. Cooper was alive, he was now a free man.

And not a single dollar of the ransom money had ever turned up. If Cooper was a corpse in the mountains, the money was there with him, just waiting to be found.

Most of the population of Portland and Seattle seemed to catch 'Cooper fever' and the hills were alive with the sound of marching feet. But they scoured the mountains in vain.

The fever subsided until 1979 when a solitary deer hunter in the dense forest above the village of Kelso, Washington, stumbled across a man-made intrusion in the virgin forest. It was a thick plastic warning sign from the tail door hatch of a Boeing 727. Its futile message read: 'This hatch must remain firmly locked in flight.'

Overnight the village became a boom town as thousands of amateur sleuths stormed the peaks trying to find Cooper's treasure one step ahead of the FBI teams who descended by helicopter. Astrologers, mapmakers and local tourist guides made almost as much money as Cooper's missing loot from the hopeful punters.

'The mountains were almost trampled flat by the crowds,' admitted State Police Inspector Walter Wagner. 'But none of us found a thing.'

Had Cooper got clean away with all the cash?

That riddle was partially solved seven and a half years after the hijacking.

Industrial painter Harold Ingram and his son Brian, eight, were wading along the sandy shore of the Columbia River just outside the Washington state border when they stirred up a bundle of weathered banknotes from the river bank.

The money amounted to about $3,000 of Cooper's cash, according to one of the 30 FBI men who cordoned off the Ingrams' family picnic site and fought off the new wave of treasure seekers.

Scientific tests on the bank notes and the mud caked around them showed that the money had probably been washed downstream six years before from an area 80 km (50 miles) upstream – on any one of hundreds of tributaries higher up the mountain range.

The hunters vanished over the rocky skyline, sawing and digging their way through the forests once more.

'That's the closest we ever came to him,' Special Agent John Pringle of the FBI reported. 'But we are still looking for an invisible needle in a mountain range of haystacks.'

If D. B. Cooper is still alive, he can freely identify himself to the FBI now. The legal time limit on his crime means he will never face a criminal prosecution for the Thanksgiving Day hijacking. But there is probably one big obstacle which could prevent the world's only successful skyjacker from coming forward . . .

The FBI may have given up, but at the offices of the Internal Revenue in the nation's capital in Washington DC the file on D. B. Cooper remains open forever.

The skyjacker faces a bill for $300,000 – more than his ransom haul – and a 10-year jail sentence for failing to file income tax returns.

The taxman explained:

'We tax illegal money just as we tax legal money; it's all income as far as we are concerned.

D. B. Cooper became $200,000 dollars richer after the hijack and he never paid his tax on that money. Now he owes us interest on that sum and penalty payments. We have assessed his tax liability as a bachelor with no dependants and no additional source of income. If he wants to arrange an appointment with our auditors to claim some allowances and expenses we will be happy to meet him.

Until then we are still looking for Mr D. B. Cooper, and his assets. There is no Statute of Limitations for tax dodgers.'

The Canine Sherlock Holmes

It stands, just over 0.3 m (1 ft) high, as the ultimate, golden goal of some of the world's greatest sporting stars. Whether held high in triumph or simply coveted from afar, the Jules Rimet Trophy is the prize of prizes in the field of professional soccer.

It has embraced the dreams of hundreds of nations, of legendary players such as the great Pele and of literally millions of waving, cheering fanatics from all corners of the globe.

It is more commonly known as the World Cup – a once-in-a-lifetime reward every four years to one country and its eleven most gifted, idolized footballers.

Such is the occasion of its presentation that it is passed into the hands of the football players only from those of kings and queens, presidents and prime ministers.

When it was brought to England a few weeks before the start of the 1966 World Cup tournament it was promptly stolen. The cup over which rival countries had, through the years, fought so bitterly – even off the playing field and in the political arena – was pilfered from a stamp exhibition at London's Central Hall, Westminster, where it had been on display. It was considered an international scandal.

Scotland Yard was summoned immediately. Questions were asked in parliaments around the world. Huge rewards from all sorts of organizations were offered for the cup's safe return. Outside England the mood was hostile and angry, especially in those nations where soccer seems almost to vie with religion for the hearts and souls of the people. No cost or effort was to be spared to restore not only a football trophy, but also national pride, to its rightful place.

The police who had been ordered in hot pursuit of the World Cup thief or thieves found themselves on a cold trail. The trophy had, apparently, vanished into thin air and the hunt for clues or suspects was a bitterly frustrating one. It was unlikely that anyone would have stolen the cup simply to melt it down. The actual gold content was then worth only about £2,000 despite the fact that it was insured for £30,000. The real value, however, was priceless.

Private collectors, undaunted by dealing on the black market to procure their secret hoards of treasure, would have paid a fortune to have the legendary cup in a hidden vault. That was the only theory on which the beleaguered police could pin any hope.

For a fortnight in early March 1966, the world held its breath as the desperate search for the stolen cup continued in vain. It was a tragedy of enormous proportions to dedicated followers of football. But, more than that, it was an almighty embarrassment to England, which was playing host to the prestigious tournament for the first time in its sporting history.

It was vital that the cup was found immediately.

Screaming newspaper headlines posed all sorts of questions, some of them unthinkable to the hierarchy of FIFA, soccer's world governing body ... Was it in the hands of an unscrupulous millionaire? Was it stolen and then simply thrown away to be lost forever when the thief realized the enormity of his crime? Was it being held by a syndicate of villains, waiting to sell it off to the highest bidder?

Had it, been melted down or destroyed? The possibilities were endless.

The answer came, in the most unexpected – and rather unglamorous – way on the night of 19 March.

David Corbett, a 26-year-old Thames lighterman, was taking a family dog, Pickles, for a walk near his home in Beulah Hill, Norwood, South London, when, out of the corner of his eye, he spotted a glint, a reflection that lasted for just a split second.

It had come from what had appeared to be a bundle of dirty old newspapers under a laurel bush that Pickles, a cross-bred collie, had been sniffing and pawing at with great interest. Mr Corbett called to his dog. But Pickles would not come.

As David Corbett recalled later:

'I bent under the bush, lifted the top layer of newspapers, and there it was. I knew what it was at once. It was the World Cup.

I think that the first thing I actually saw was an inscription on the cup. The words 'Brazil 1962' were written near the base. I'm a keen football fan and I had been following all the reports in the newspapers. You can imagine how absolutely taken aback I was.

I took it back to our flat to show my wife Jeannie and then we phoned the police, who were as astounded as we were. Yet the truth is that I would not have given the old bundle of newspapers it was wrapped in a sideways glance or a second thought if it hadn't been for Pickles. He was the real hero of the hour.'

Indeed he was. Animal lovers from all over the world began to shower gifts on the canine sleuth. England's National Canine Defence League bestowed

Pickles and his owner at the *Café Royal* with Henry Cooper

on him its highest honour: a silver medal inscribed with the words 'To Pickles, for his part in the recovery of the World Cup, 1966.' At the ceremony at which it was presented, the league's secretary enthused: 'Pickles, by his action, has given prominence to the canine world and so helped us in our task.'

At the same ceremony – and there were many others for the 'furry Sherlock Holmes' as he was dubbed – a hotel pageboy stepped up with a silver salver of further gifts. There was a rubber bone, £53, collected among the hotel's staff – and the best steak for him to eat.

Pickles, oblivious to the importance of the occasion, simply lay down and yawned.

But the still unanswered question was: who actually stole the World Cup? It was a question, despite a number of suspicions, that the police were never to answer.

Yet, as in all unsolved crimes, when the finger of suspicion is pointed, however wrongly, there are people who are bound to suffer. That, amazingly, was the sad plight of none other than Pickles' owner, Mr Corbett. Less than two months after his alertness helped recover the prized trophy, Mr Corbett told a newspaper:

'I wish I'd never seen the damn thing. I was quite excited about it at the time but I seem to have had nothing but trouble since.

When I gave it to the police, they appeared at first not to believe my story about Pickles finding it under a laurel bush. They grilled me. They asked me where I was on the day the cup was stolen, whether I collected stamps, if I had ever been to Central Hall, Westminster, and so on.

Eventually, they believed me. But the trouble didn't end with the police. Ordinary people have been suspecting me of having had something to do with the theft of the cup. My wife and I were in Trafalgar Square and a group of boys saw us. They shouted at me: "He's the one who stole it. Let's drown the dog in the fountain." It was terrible.'

In the end, of course, Mr Corbett was completely vindicated – and received rewards totalling more than £6,000. He did not watch the World Cup itself, but he did join in the spirit of Pickles's success when he allowed the dog to be taken to meet each member of the West German final team – all of whom touched him for luck, hoping they would find the cup theirs at the end of the football match.

But it was not to be. England took the trophy and, thanks to Pickles, who sadly died only four years later, erased memories of the most embarrassing episode in soccer history.

The Missing Murderers

It is more than half a century since Adolf Hitler brought the Nazis to power in Germany. Just 12 years later they were vanquished, leaving behind the evidence of what has been called the greatest crime in history: the annihilation of Europe's Jews.

The Nazis also left behind a maze of mysteries – a criminal enigma of as great a magnitude as the crime itself. For the full story of the massacre of millions of Jews can never be told until all the missing culprits are brought to account. Only then will the question marks that still hang over history's most shameful act ever be removed.

Many of the mysteries surrounding Hitler's attempted genocide were answered when his death-camp supremo, Adolf Eichmann, was captured by the world's chief Nazi hunter Simon Wiesenthal. But Eichmann's trial and execution did nothing to stop the heated debate that continues to this day about how many of those in German government, judiciary, armed forces and civil service knew and condoned the dreadful pogrom.

In 1983 a few more pieces were fitted into the jigsaw after Klaus Barbie, the wartime Gestapo chief in Lyons, was extradited from Bolivia to face trial in France. It was the excuse for Dr Wiesenthal to update his list of the most wanted Nazis still at large.

Asked why, at the age of 76, he still pursued them from his Jewish Documentation Centre in Vienna, Wiesenthal said:

'When history looks back on this century I want people to know that the Nazis were not able to kill 11 million people and get away with it. Mine is the last organization in the world still hunting the Nazis. If I stopped, the Nazis and history would say, "The Jews gave up."'

Wiesenthal's list at that time named the ten most wanted Nazis, whom he placed in order of responsibility for crime as well as actual criminal activity. He said: 'I have a compact with the dead. If I could get all ten it would be an achievement. Sometimes I think if I could just get Josef Mengele my soul would finally be at peace.'

At that time, Wiesenthal believed he had located Dr Mengele, No. 3 on his list and known as the 'Angel of Death' of Auschwitz. But Mengele, said to be living in a remote Mennonite religious community on the border of Bolivia and Paraguay, was thought to be impossible to extradite. He was reported to be a registered refugee and a Paraguayan citizen.

The escaped Nazi leaders have now grown old, however, and despite Dr Wiesenthal's patient efforts, death rather than justice is more likely to catch up with these ten killers in hiding ...

1. Heinrich Mueller: Chief of the Gestapo.

Mueller was known as the killer with the fountain pen. He would never kill anyone himself. He only wrote out the orders. He very seldom visited a concentration camp or a gas chamber or an execution.

A World War 1 Army officer, he joined the Bavarian police and only in 1939 the Nazi party – out of necessity rather than belief. Hard-working, he always sheltered under the orders of others, beginning his instructions 'the Reichsführer has ordered' this or that. His industrious, low-profile, comradely but never friendly character led to his appointment as Gestapo general.

Although he himself never killed anybody, he was responsible for the deaths of millions of Jews, prisoners and hostages. He knew every detail about the concentration camps, could quote statistics about inmates and even the death rate at notorious camps like Auschwitz. The bureaucratic killer vanished at the end of World War 2, was thought to have died in the Berlin street fighting. But when his grave was opened three skulls were found. Not one of them was Mueller's.

Since then, the Nazi hunters have followed leads that he went over to the Russians, then moved on to Albania. Others tracked him to Spain, then Suez and in 1963 he was confidently identified as a resident in Cairo, safe from the Israelis. Israeli agents were arrested in Frau Mueller's home in Munich but they found no lead to his whereabouts.

His aliases include Jan Belinski, Pole; Amin Abdel Megid and Alfred Mardes, Arab. Officially, his fate and whereabouts are unknown.

2. Richard Gluecks: Inspector-general of all concentration camps.

Less is known about Gluecks than about most Nazi war criminals, except that he was a Gruppenführer, head of the administration bureau of the RHSA, the Reich Security Head Office in overall control of concentration camps.

In 1938, 20,000 Jews were sent to 'protective custody' in these camps. By 1939 six major camps had been established, including the notorious Dachau, Buchenwald and Ravensbrück. Eight others were to follow in the next three years including the most notorious, Auschwitz, where more than a million people died. Gluecks, who ordered deportations and managed the network of camps, vanished without trace. His fate and whereabouts are unknown.

3. Dr Josef Mengele: Chief Medical Officer, Auschwitz concentration camp.

Mengele was accused of being directly responsible for the deaths of 400,000 people. A medical graduate of both Frankfurt and Munich universities – both of which have cancelled his academic qualifications – he was known as 'The Angel of Death' to Auschwitz concentration camp.

As the prisoners filed through the main gate, beneath the sign 'Work Makes Men Free', Mengele would prod them with his stick and order them to be worked to death, to undergo hideous experiments or to be taken directly to the gas chambers. All the time, a band played on.

One of his experiments, aimed at proving Hitler's theory that Germans were a super-race, was to alter the hair and eyes of victims by genetic manipulation. Many who did not die were blinded.

He escaped from West Germany after the war, travelled to Italy and then Argentina, before settling in Paraguay where he became a naturalized citizen in 1973. He took out citizenship papers largely because West Germany, and the Nazi hunters, had located him and were offering vast sums of money in reward for his return.

Mengele had to remain constantly on the move, unable to sleep in the same bed for more than two weeks at a time.

At the end of 1978 and early 1979 his fellow Nazis put about the story that Mengele was dead in order to protect the strong war criminal colony in Paraguay. They even circulated pictures of Mengele on the mortuary slab showing the scar on his right arm where his tattooed ss number had been removed. It was, in fact, the body of ss Captain Eduardo Roschmann who sent 80,000 Jews to their deaths at the concentration camp at Riga, Latvia.

As a Paraguayan citizen, Mengele continued to live in that country under goverment protection.

4. Walter Rauff: Commander of a unit which provided gas trucks for concentration camps.

Rauff is accused of being responsible, directly and indirectly, for the deaths of 250,000 people – despite the fact that there is little evidence of direct contact between Rauff and his victims.

He was 'the ambulance chief'. His transports looked like ordinary Red Cross ambulances into which Jews and others regarded as racially undesirable were herded. But they were not taken to hospital, as their guards promised. Once inside the 'ambulances', the doors were locked and the guards opened the valves on cylinders attached to the vehicles. The passengers were gassed to death.

According to Weisenthal in 1983, Rauff is alive and well in Chile where he openly ran a meat freezing factory. He was even known to answer letters addressed to him in Punta Arenas, but goverment protection ensured he was not molested.

At one time Dr Wiesenthal pleaded with Dr Henry Kissinger, then American's roving ambassador, to help secure Rauff's extradition. Dr Kissinger, himself a Jew and of German origin, declined because he could not interfere without compromising himself and his country diplomatically.

Rauff, like Mengele, has been used in a number of works of fiction including Frederick Forsyth's famous novel, *The Odessa File*. But his real post-war existence in South America has been stranger than fiction. Both Mengele and Rauff have been suspected of drug racketeering. The Chileans have had to deny a number of stories about Rauff, notably that the Chilean government was employing him as an anti-Communist agent.

The government at one time denied that Rauff was living in Chile ... but the former ss colonel's own letters were ample proof to the contary.

5. Anton Burger: Field officer and assistant to Adolf Eichmann, head of the Gestapo's Department of Jewish Affairs.

Burger was deputy commander of Theresienstadt concentration camp, on the Czech-German border. The 'model' camp was used to dispel stories of Nazi atrocities. It was even opened to neutral visitors to show that stories about the concentration camps were simply Allied propaganda. But behind the scenes, the inmates of Theresienstadt were subject to 'experiments'. Some were to be poisoned. Women were forced to undergo abortions to prevent the increase of the Jewish race. Others were sterilized.

In the hunt for Nazi war criminals Anton Burger was often mistaken for Wilhelm Burger, chief administrator at Auschwitz.

In 1948 Anton Burger escaped from the prison where he was awaiting trial. In the search which ensued the authorities eventually arrested Wilhelm Burger, accused for his part in ordering lorry loads of gas with which to murder Jews at Auschwitz.

Wilhelm was jailed for eight years – but because he had spent eight years in a Polish prison he was freed. Anton vanished and his whereabouts are unknown.

6. Rolf Guenther: Deputy to Adolf Eichmann.

Rolf and his brother, Hans, were both ss majors but it was Rolf, the quiet one, who was entrusted with carrying out Hitler's programme for exterminating the Jews.

When Eichmann was kidnapped in Argentina and returned to Israel to be tried, he accused Guenther of taking a personal initiative in the death camps and of carrying out some orders behind his back. He insisted that Guenther must have had and acted on special orders direct from Mueller, by-passing Eichmann.

The truth was that Guenther had been chosen as Eichmann's second in command because he would willingly carry out the 'final solution' to the Jewish problem. He was sent to remove all Jews from Denmark. He visited Greece, Hungary and other countries as an expert on 'the Jewish problem'.

Ample documentation proves that Guenther had a confidential instruction to arrange sterilization, medical experiments and the gassing of inmates.

Guenther disappeared at the end of the war. His whereabouts are unknown.

7. Alois Brunner: Another of Eichmann's assistants.

According to Wiesenthal's files, Brunner is specially responsible for the deaths of thousands of Jews in Czechoslovakia and Greece.

Like Guenther, he worked for Eichmann in the 'Jewish Museum', a propaganda section at the head office of the Nazi Party. He then moved to the Jewish section of the Gestapo and early in the war was appointed field officer in France.

There he arranged the deportation of, at first, stateless Jews, then foreign Jews and finally French Jews. They were taken to local concentration camps and then mostly to Auschwitz.

As in the case of Guenther, Eichmann tried to maintain that once Brunner had left him to visit some other country he was out of Eichmann's jurisdiction. But Eichmann, who was not believed, and was hanged for his war crimes, left behind considerable evidence, which helps condemn Brunner.

Yet, according to Wiesenthal, in 1983 Brunner was living under Arab protection in Damascus, Syria, under the name of Dr Fisher.

8. Josef Schwamberger: Another of Eichmann's assistants, former commander of the Jewish ghetto at Przemysl, Poland.

Before the war about 500,000 Jews lived in Galicia, Poland. Then the Germans came and herded them into ghettos. Schwamberger is thought to have been responsible for the deaths of 15,000 of them. The Warsaw ghetto, where there was bloody revolt, uprising and suppression, was the most infamous. But there were many others.

After the war, Schwamberger, a member of the so-called Odessa escape group, fled to Italy and then to Argentina, where Nazis still received asylum. Despite denials as to his presence, Argentinian police arrested him in 1973 after requests by West Germany that he be extradited.

The powerful group of Nazis resident there intervened. The request was refused – and he was released.

9. Dr Aribert Heim: Director of the concentration camp at Mauthausen, Austria.

In February 1941, the Germans made their first mass arrests in Holland by rounding up 400 Jews in Amsterdam and sending them first to Buchenwald and then to Mauthausen. The Red Cross revealed that only one survived.

The camp's 'death book', found by the Allies, revealed 35,318 deaths, a total which compared with camps like Dachau and Buchenwald.

The inmates had a saying that if you reached Mauthausen, Dr Heim would 'look after you'. The grim truth was that many were taken from the notorious Auschwitz on a death march to Mauthausen. Some survived that march –

only to be sent on another to Zeltenlager.

One witness who survived both marches said they were so hungry that when the Allies bombed the area he 'saw people eating human flesh, the flesh of victims of the air raid'.

After the war Dr Heim vanished. His whereabouts are unknown.

10. Friedrich Wartzog: Commander of the Lemberg-Janowska concentration camp, Russia, formerly Poland.

Wartzog is accused of ordering the killing of 40,000 people. Some of the worst evidence against him was given on oath by Eichmann at his trial, when he talked of 'a spring of blood gushing from the earth' where executed Jews had been buried at Lemberg-Janowska.

Prisoners were kept without food for three days, existed on grass and then if found unfit were shot. One hobby of the guards was shooting at the prisoners as they went to work – at their ears, noses, fingers. If they were badly injured an executioner would finish them off.

Wartzog, who presided, escaped. His whereabouts are unknown.

France's Uncrowned King

Before the revolutions of peasants and elected parliaments began to sweep through Europe in the 18th and 19th centuries, the royal dynasties of kings and princes jealously guarded their awesome power with strict codes of bloodline and heritage and succession.

The rulers who claimed a God-given right to govern millions of subjects, built their fabulous fortunes on elaborate rules of royal lineage. Loyal courtiers were always on hand to advise on the interpretation of the laws of succession in the tangled web of regal inter-marriage, first-born sons, feuding cousins and charlatan pretenders to great thrones and titles.

Often when powerful monarchs passed from the gilded stage and their relatives fell to squabbling among themselves, the line of succession could pass the mantle of power to tiny babies, first-born crown princes not old enough to walk or talk.

Jealous royal power brokers would often cast an envious eye on the cradle of some child-king, knowing that in many cases a quirk of fate, like a bout of fatal chicken pox, could swing an empire into the hands of a rival relative.

Sometimes they were not slow to realize the advantages of giving fate a helping hand. Snatching a kingdom from a child, taking the royal candy from a baby, was fair game, even if the infant was a close blood relative.

When little Charles Louis was born into the royal family of Bourbon in 1785, he seemed set for a life of luxury. He was the younger of two royal children, but as the male heir, the Dauphin, he took priority over his older sister Marie Thérèse. His destiny was to rule France as the inheritor of its palaces and grand estates. But the overburdened French peasants had other ideas. Louis was only four years old when the Revolution burst on to the streets of Paris and the mobs began to howl for an end to monarchy.

The little Dauphin's parents, Louis XVI and Marie Antoinette, whose free spending lifestyle had so outraged their poverty stricken subjects, were soon prisoners of the Revolution. For two years Louis and Marie and their children were kept under house arrest as French democracy went through its own turbulent infancy, ruling the country in a confusion of committees and assemblies.

Luck ran out for King Louis and his Queen in 1793 during the session of the newly appointed Convention which unleashed the infamous Reign of Terror. Louis and Marie became just two of the stream of doomed French nobility whose lives were ended by the guillotine.

While the members of the Convention transferred the little Dauphin and his sister to the Temple Prison in Paris, the exiled royalists who had fled abroad immediately proclaimed the seven-year-old boy their new King, Louis XVII.

There is little doubt that many of the fiery members of the new Republic's National Assembly would happily have guillotined the boy king and his sister. But they could not overlook his potential as a pawn in the bargaining game they had to play with their hostile neighbours of Austria, Prussia and Spain, where the ruling royal families, fought frequent invasion skirmishes with the French to try to restore the monarchy. As long as the Dauphin and his sister remained prisoners in the Temple, their continued safe-keeping had some value if the National Assembly used them as hostages to buy off the pressure from threatening outsiders.

In the meantime, the royalists in exile and their sympathizers inside Paris, began a whole series of plots to free the bewildered little Dauphin by bribery or subterfuge.

Even some National Assembly members, worried that the Revolution might be short-lived, considered smuggling the Dauphin to their own secret hideaways to bargain for their own lives if the royalists ever regained the upper hand. Soon all Paris was abuzz with rumours that the Dauphin had been spirited out of the temple to become a youthful figurehead for a Royalist revival.

Louis XVII

To quell the speculation, the National Assembly appointed a team of guardians and commissoners to make regular visits to the Temple to check the well-being of the Dauphin and his sister, and to report back to them.

A puzzling report was recorded after a visit on 19 December 1794, when National Assembly member Harmand inspected the nine-year-old boy in his cell at the Temple. He noted he met a child in poor health, suffering from a disabling swelling on his arms and legs. The most bizarre aspect was the boy's responses to Harmand's inquiries about his treatment. The boy showed no signs of hearing his questions and never uttered a sound in reply. He was totally deaf and dumb. Harmond's report was quickly hushed up.

In May 1795, the boy in the Temple became seriously ill and doctors were ordered to attend him. The health of the boy, apparently still a deaf mute, deteriorated still further until the night of 8 June when he died.

Four doctors authorized by the Committee of Public Safety carried out a quick autopsy on the dead boy, removing his heart and dissecting his head. They diagnosed the cause of death as scrofula, tuberculosis of the glands of the neck.

But they never carried out an formal identification of him by his sister, Marie Thérèse, who had been kept prisoner for two years in another cell on the other side of the Temple. The body, the head swathed in bandages, was placed in a coffin and hustled off for burial in a common grave in the churchyard of Sainte Marguérite.

The next day, amid continuing rumours that another child had been switched for the Dauphin in the Temple, the Convention announced his death without making any further comment.

And so the royal house of Bourbon seemed doomed to wither as the French Republic embarked on a new era of its history under the leadership of a dynamic young Army officer from Corsica, Napoleon Bonaparte.

Napoleon took less than a decade of glorious military conquest before he tried to found his own royal dynasty, crowning himself Emperor and handing out royal titles to his own children, brothers and friends.

But after his defeat at Waterloo in 1815, the victorious allies decided it was time for real royalty to regain the throne of France. Their choice was the brother of the guillotined Louis XVI, the uncle of the Dauphin. The new monarch, next in line after the boy-king who had never ruled, became Louis XVIII. It was the sign for resurrected Dauphins to pop up all over Europe.

Dozens of 'dauphins', all about the right age of 30 and all well versed in the folklore of the alleged switch in the Temple, put forward their claims and where exposed as blatant frauds.

The most curious claim came 15 years later from a Prussian watchmaker living in London. In 1830, when another Revolution, less bloody and violent, had swept the royal family of Bourbon off the French throne of France yet again watchmaker Karl Wilhelm Naundorff came forward. He insisted he did not want to try to rule France, only to prove himself to be the missing Dauphin and to try to benefit from what little privilege was still attached to the title.

Naundorff gave a long, detailed account of how he recalled 35 years earlier being carried out of the Temple on 8 June, 1795, after being drugged with opium, and spending the next 14 years being passed from 'safe house' to 'safe house' in France, England and Germany. In 1800, he claimed, the King of Prussia had organized false identity papers for him in the name of Karl Naundorff. He then married and settled down, after serving a short prison term for counterfeiting coins.

In 1833 in France, Naundorff organized a meeting with Madame Rambaud, the dead Dauphin's former nanny, and Vicomte de la Rochefoucauld, an emissary from the Dauphin's sister, then Duchess of Angoulême. The nanny was convinced about his identity and the Vicomte reported that he was very impressed with Naundorff's claims and the watchmaker's striking physical resemblance to his 'father', the dead King Louis XVI.

But the Duchess, the Dauphin's sister, took no notice until 1836 when Naundorff tried to force her into a civil court case to prove his claim. He was arrested by French authorities and deported back to England. At home in London he set about pressing his claim, in an exhaustively researched book published later that year.

All copies of the book sent to France were seized by French customs officials at Calais. Naundorff continued to bombard the French authorities and the Duchess with petitions, undeterred by an attempt on his life at his home in Clarence Place, London. He was shot, literally with his pants down, in the outdoor toilet in his garden. He survived the wound and a Frenchman was later arrested and charged with the attack.

Two other attempts were made on his life in 1841 as Naundorff struggled to earn a living as an inventor of artillery weapons. He was badly burned in a deliberate explosion in his workshop and another arson attack on his home later that year.

With his business burned out, Karl Naundorff was bankrupt and spent four years in the grim Newgate debtor's prison in London.

Released in 1845, he travelled to Holland to try to interest the Dutch government in his designs for a new field gun. Before negotiations were complete, Naundorff died on 10 August.

The official Dutch death certificate identified him as Charles Louis de Bourbon, Duke of Normandy, Louis XVII, aged 60, son of Louis XVI and Marie Antoinette. The Dutch doctor who performed the routine autopsy noted his body bore certain marks – a mole on the thigh, triangular vaccination marks on his arm and a scar on his upper lip. The marks correspond exactly to the descriptions given by Madame Rambaud, the governess to the Dauphin Louis from his birth until 1792, the year before he was locked away in the Temple.

If Karl Naundorff was indeed the young Dauphin, the leaders of the French Revolution who locked him away as a child, without trial or charge, denied him his heritage and his chance to change the course of history.

But if his story was true, which cruel and heartless conspirators, royalists or double-crossing revolutionaries, snatched him from the Temple and left a terrified deaf mute boy to die of disease and maltreatment in solitary confinement in his place?

The Sinking of the *Salem*

The 96,000 ton supertanker *Salem* was a floating time bomb, in danger of erupting into a massive fire-ball at any moment. But her captain, officers and 18 crewmen were calm, apparently refusing to panic, waiting quietly on deck and scanning the horizon for passing ships.

On 17 January 1979, the Greek captain of the *Salem* noted in his log that the ship had been rocked by a series of explosions which had left it floating helpless and without engines in the Atlantic Ocean 160 km (100 miles) off the African coast of Senegal.

The ship's log also noted with relief that the mysterious explosions and small fires had failed to ignite any of the brimming cargo of 200,000 tons of volatile Kuwaiti crude oil which packed the tanker's holds.

The *Salem* remained afloat for another 30 hours. Almost inevitably in the busy shipping lanes, she was spotted by the tanker *British Trident*, outward bound from England and headed for the same Persian Gulf terminal the *Salem* had left more than a month before. Twenty minutes after the *British Trident* first sighted the *Salem*, the British ship recorded the first and only distress radio call from the stricken ship.

As *British Trident* turned to answer the SOS call a bright cloud of orange smoke billowed up from the *Salem*. But there was no need for the rescuers to approach too close. Within 30 minutes the *Salem*'s powerful lifeboats had met them halfway. The British sailors could only marvel at the *Salem*'s crew, unhurried and magnificently composed in the face of awesome danger, as they filed aboard the *British Trident* in an orderly queue, with their suitcases neatly packed.

The ship had survived a day and a night still afloat although listing slightly. With reasonable luck it could be presumed that the *Salem* might survive a lot longer, even long enough to put a damage repair and salvage crew aboard.

But within ten minutes of her crew being rescued, the *Salem*'s bows dipped below the swell and she sank out of sight.

The crew of the *British Trident* were relieved when the potential fire-bomb slipped below the waves. Now they put their own tanker's engines full ahead to get well clear of the catastrophic fountain of oil which would gush to the surface from the *Salem*'s hold. They knew that the *Salem*'s massive cargo, valued at £25 million, was likely to produce one of the worst oil slicks the world had ever known.

Almost as a warning of the impending pollution disaster, one gigantic oil bubble broke the surface of the ocean. And then it stopped.

The *Salem* slipped further and further downward into the Atlantic, in water too deep for any diver to reach her. She was gone and lost for good, of that there was no doubt.

The following day the crew of the *Salem* were put ashore in Dakar, the capital of Senegal. The captain dismissed his grateful crew and prepared himself for questioning at a routine inquiry into the loss of his ship. He notified the owners of the *Salem*, a newly formed shipping company sharing the same accommodation address in Monrovia, Liberia, as 200 other shipping owners, that their vessel had foundered. He informed the owners of the oil, Shell International Trading in London, that their valuable cargo had been lost and compensation would have to come from the insurers.

The skipper carefully filed his own insurance claim, £12 million for the cost of the *Salem*, less than half the value of its cargo. Then, as soon as the Senegal authorities agreed to release him, he flew home to Athens.

As insurance investigators began to unravel some of the unexplained causes of the sinking of the *Salem*, one of the tanker's crew added a new twist to the riddle.

The crewman, a Tunisian, turned up in Paris, spending money like water. He claimed that the money he flung so recklessly around the nightclubs came from a bonus of thousands of Swiss francs paid by the owners of the *Salem*.

And that bonus, he claimed, was paid to all the crewmen who entered into a conspiracy of silence a few days after the *Salem* left the Kuwaiti oil loading terminal at Mena Al Ahmdi and cleared the Persian Gulf. The high living crewman boasted that the shadowy businessmen who owned the *Salem* had bluffed their way into a fortune by offering their services to carry the cargo of oil from Kuwait to England.

The Kuwaiti oil would have been worth double its value to one group of customers 3,220 km (2,000 miles) away, the industries of South Africa. Most Arab oil exporters maintain a united anti-apartheid policy against the South African regime and refuse to sell them any of their output. South Africa buys its oil wherever and whenever it can – and pays top price.

The crewman insisted that this ship made a secret rendezvous with a South African tanker off the Cape of Good Hope, transferred its precious cargo and then partially flooded its tanks to prevent it riding suspiciously high in the water. Then it continued its journey as part of an elaborate charade. It sank conveniently off Senegal, its nearest point to land after leaving South African waters.

In Athens the skipper of the *Salem* dismissed his crewman's uncorroborated allegations as a sailor's yarn, meant to add spice and intrigue to a sad but perfectly plausible explanation for the loss of the tanker. The South African government maintained a discreet silence.

But insurance investigators were already suspicious that the *Salem* had taken more than a month to reach the Senegal coast after leaving Kuwait. It should have made that part of its journey in only three weeks. The time gap, many of them claim, can only be explained by an unscheduled detour somewhere along the route.

It is unlikely that anyone will ever be able to solve the riddle of the ship which seemed to sink on cue. The wreck of the *Salem* lies deep beneath the stormy waters of the Atlantic Ocean. Are its cargo tanks filled with £25 million worth of oil, seeping away quietly and unnoticed? Or are they filled with nothing more than sea water?

A Peer's Great Gamble

When Veronica, Lady Lucan, ran hysterical and bloodstained from her home in Lower Belgrave Street, Belgravia, London, on the night of 7 November 1974, her frantic cries for help sparked off one of the most baffling unsolved murder mysteries of the age.

Lying behind her in the elegant town house, just a stone's throw from Buckingham Palace, was the body of her children's nanny Sandra Rivett, aged 29, brutally battered to death, her body thrust into a canvas sack.

Lady Lucan reached the door of the crowded saloon bar of the nearby pub, The Plumbers Arms, and sobbed: 'Help me. Help me, I've just escaped from a murderer.'

Sandra Rivett

And the tale she told from her hospital bed to detectives a few hours later set them on the fruitless search to find her husband, John Bingham, the 7th Earl of Lucan. With bruising on her face and severe lacerations to her scalp, Lady Lucan, 26, told how she had tackled a tall, powerful maniac bent on murder.

She recalled how she had been spending a quiet evening at home with her two children – with the unexpected company of nanny Sandra who had originally been given the evening off to spend with her boyfriend. Sandra, who doted on Lady Lucan's children, had decided instead to stay in the house, in her own quarters.

Around 21.00 Sandra had popped her head round the door of Lady Lucan's lounge and offered to make a cup of tea for the family. Half an hour later when the nanny had not re-appeared, Lady Lucan walked down two floors to the kitchen, puzzled by the delay.

There she saw the shadowy figure of a man, crouched over the dead body of the nanny, bundling her lifeless form into a canvas sack.

As soon as Lady Lucan screamed, the man attacked her, beating her badly. She could not recognize the figure in the darkness, but as she struggled free and ran upstairs, she heard what she said was the unmistakable voice of her estranged husband call out after her.

Moments later, as she lay trembling on her bed, her husband was at her side, trying to comfort her. And when Lady Lucan ran from the house for help, her husband slipped away into the night.

A massive hunt immediately began for Lord Lucan. Police first checked his rented flat only a few streets away, where he had moved the previous year when he had separated from Lady Lucan and started divorce proceedings. But by that time, barely two hours after the murder, Lord Lucan had already turned up at a friend's house 72 km (45 miles) from the scene of the crime, driving a borrowed car.

There the socialite peer, a man-about-town and professional gambler, told one of his closest family friends his own version of the horror of the nanny's murder. He claimed he had been walking past his wife's home on his way to his own flat to change for dinner at one of his fashionable gambling clubs and saw through the venetian blinds of the basement kitchen what looked like a man attacking Lady Lucan.

'I let myself in with my own key and rushed down to protect her,' Lucan told his friend. 'I slipped on a pool of blood and the attacker ran off. My wife was hysterical and accusing me of being her attacker.'

Despite his denial, Lord Lucan never stayed around to confirm his version of events to the police – or to anyone else. The day after the murder, his car, which carried a portion of the same lead pipe which had been used to kill

Lord and Lady Lucan

Sandra Rivett, was found abandoned at Newhaven, Sussex, a port with a regular ferry service to France.

Police began a thorough check of Lucan's aristocratic friends in England, suspecting that wealthy socialites might be shielding him. But all lines of inquiry petered out.

A year later the coroner's inquest into the death of the nanny weighed up all the evidence and took the unusual step of officially recording her death as murder – and naming Lord Lucan as the man who had committed the murder. English law was changed shortly after that judgement to ensure that never again could anyone be named as a murderer until they were found, charged, tried and found guilty under normal criminal procedure.

Seven years after the murder, when Lucan had vanished without touching any of his bank accounts, without surrendering himself, and still undiscovered by any of the police searches which spread from Africa to America, the fugitive peer was declared legally dead.

The two policemen who led the search have both retired from Scotland Yard, still arguing about the unsolved crime. Superintendent Roy Ransom, who studied every single statement and grilled scores of witnesses, maintained: 'He killed the nanny by mistake, thinking he could dispose of his wife and get the custody of the children he loved. When he realized the error, he killed himself in some remote spot, like a lord and a gentleman.'

But Superintendent Dave Gerring, who supervised the same murder hunt, concluded: 'Lucan is still in hiding somewhere and he is the only man who knows the full story. He is a lord and a gentleman, but he is still a gambler. And he is still gambling on the odds that no one will ever find him.'

Suspect Deceased

The finger of suspicion pointed unwaveringly at Graham Sturley. He was the classic murder suspect. The 37-year-old former private detective had certainly studied case histories of people who had vanished and never been seen alive again. And when Linda, his own wife, went missing, Sturley had the know-how, the motive and the opportunity to have murdered her.

METROPOLITAN POLICE
Appeal for Assistance

AP/23A/82

MISSING

Mrs Linda Jacqueline STURLEY, 5'4" tall with shoulder length, fair hair and aged 29, left her home in Main Road, Biggin Hill, Kent, between 9pm on Friday 17 July and Saturday 18 July, 1981.

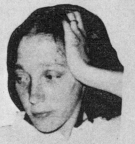

She was 6 months pregnant. She was last seen wearing a blue maternity dress.

DO YOU KNOW HER?
HAVE YOU SEEN HER RECENTLY?
DO YOU HAVE ANY OTHER INFORMATION?

Please contact the Police at
CATFORD POLICE STATION
Tel: 01-697 9502
All information treated as strictly confidential

The detectives who first called at his home in Biggin Hill, Kent, were quickly convinced that Sturley, earning a living as a property developer, had killed his petite, unfaithful 29-year-old wife. He openly admitted to them his hatred for her flaunted love affairs with other men.

But the police began their investigation with one great disadvantage. Linda Sturley had been missing for 12 months by the time her worried mother, Mrs Ada Webb, walked into her local police station and reported her daughter's disappearance. She had been stalled long enough by assurances from son-in-law Sturley that, although Linda had left home, she had been in touch with him by telephone.

When the police arrived on the doorstep of Sturley's neat suburban bungalow he told them frankly: 'Yes, she's gone and I don't expect to see her again. I don't know where she is and I'm glad to get rid of her.'

Then the detectives began to piece together the facts.

Linda Sturley had last been seen at her home in July 1981, when her sister visited her. Tearfully Linda, who was six months pregnant, confessed that her husband had beaten her and punched her in the stomach during a violent argument the night before, when he raged that one of her lovers was the father of the child she was expecting.

The next day Linda, a pretty and vivacious sales representative for the Avon cosmetics company, vanished.

The Sturleys' home

Graham Sturley

With an air of finality, Sturley had told his two children, a six-year-old girl and a four-year-old boy, that their mother would never be returning. Neighbours noticed that Sturley had a garden bonfire, burning a complete wardrobe of his wife's clothes. And for the next year, until July 1982, Sturley lived as if Linda had simply gone away.

He even telephoned his wife's family to reassure them that Linda was still well, at the same time as someone with a detailed knowledge of the missing woman's bank passbooks had forged her signature to take everything out of her savings accounts and cash cheques for her maternity benefit payments.

Linda Sturley's family doctor revealed that the missing woman would need to give birth to her baby by Caesarian operation. Government health officials checked the records of every maternity hospital and clinic in Britain and no patient answering her description had been admitted.

And the police discovered that her jealous husband had even used the techniques of his former detective agency to tap his own telephone and record conversations between Linda and her lovers.

'We know your wife had a string of lovers and she was a bad wife,' one policeman told Sturley sympathetically. 'And we understand that sometimes pressure like that can drive a man to murder.'

But Sturley, who had a history of poor health and heart ailments, never faltered once during long sessions of police interrogation. 'You think I have buried her in the garden,' he accused bitterly. 'Well I wouldn't have been so silly, that would have poisoned the flowers.'

It was only a matter of time, police thought, before they found Linda Sturley's body and broke through her husband's brooding, angry defiance to gain a confession.

Sturley, unshakeably refusing to admit any part in his wife's disappearance, told them: 'She had walked out on me so many times in the past I didn't bother to report her as a missing person. I'm glad she's gone, I never want to see her again.'

When intense publicity in national newspapers and on TV and radio failed to bring any response from the missing woman, the search began in earnest for Linda Sturley's body.

The floorboards were ripped up in the living room of Sturley's house and the brickwork of walls probed for hidden cavities. Infra-red and heat-seeking detection equipment was used to scan the gardens around the house and tracker teams with dogs combed the surrounding woodland and parks. Police divers plunged into lakes, streams and ponds and forensic experts were sent to examine the bones of a woman's body unearthed in a forest 48 km (30 miles) away. But there was still no sign of Linda Sturley, dead or alive.

In a series of thorough interrogations Graham Sturley taunted the police, mocking their failure at every attempt to discover the fate of his wife. Detectives, aware of his history of heart trouble, handled him with kid gloves, probing and questioning as toughly as they dared.

After three months of intensive investigation, the head of the murder inquiry squad, Detective Chief Inspector George Cressy, examined all the circumstantial evidence and decided he had enough to recommend arresting Graham Sturley and charging him with the murder of his wife.

As police legal experts began preparing the case for his arrest, confident of their prosecution and eventual conviction, Graham Sturley died of a heart attack. The murder inquiry on Linda Sturley was closed, the case file marked 'Suspect deceased'.

Graham Sturley's lawyer revealed later: 'A will was left by Mr Sturley disposing of his assests, but there was nothing dramatic in it one way or another, no confessions, no admissions.'

The Kent detectives saw no useful purpose to be served by their presence a week later at Sturley's cremation after a ceremony in the quiet chapel in Honor Oak, London.

They never saw the strange final tribute that was laid on his coffin – a wreath with the message: 'Well you got that out of the way, Sturley. All my love. . .'

The Disappearance of Goodtime Joe

With a leggy showgirl on his arm, Judge Joseph Crater stepped out of a plush nightclub on New York's 45th Street and hailed a taxi. He gave his companion an affectionate squeeze and a kiss on the cheek. 'See you tomorrow, Ruby,' said the judge, whose unorthodox social life had earned him the nickname Goodtime Joe. But he didn't. A little later, he was seen buying a theatre ticket for the Broadway hit, *Dancing Partners*.

From that moment, on 6 August 1930, Judge Joseph Crater vanished, and it happened so mysteriously and in such politically-scandalous circumstances that in America 'pulling a Crater' is still used to describe a baffling disappearance. In New York, he is still officially listed as missing, although he would now be 93 years old, and the police department still checks regular reports of sightings.

THE WORLD'S GREATEST UNSOLVED CRIMES

Judge Crater was a sentimental family man – and a womanizer on a grand scale. He was a pillar of society, yet he enjoyed the company of rogues. He believed fervently in the sanctity of the law but became part of the most corrupt administration in New York's history. He had been a brilliant professor of law at New York University, but he wanted to be rich. As a lawyer with an obvious interest in making money, he was welcomed by the city's then-shady administration. In the summer of 1929 he acted as a receiver when the bankrupt Libby Hotel was sold to a finance company for $75,000. Six weeks later, the hotel was resold to the city of New York to be demolished in a road widening scheme. The price: $2,800,000. Many members of the administration, including Crater, made a lot of money from the deal.

By 1930, he had the life-style of a very rich man. More good fortune came his way when Franklin D. Roosevelt, then Governor of New York State, made him a justice of the city's Supreme Court. Crater had finally made it. He was rich and powerful. Then, on the evening of 2 August, something happened to threaten his cosy world.

He was on holiday with his wife at their summer cottage in Maine when he received a mysterious phone call. It was enough to send the judge hurrying back to New York. 'I've got to straighten some fellows out,' was all he told his wife, promising to return for her birthday a week later. She never saw him again.

In New York on 6 August he wrote two cheques for a total of $4,100 and sent his assistant, Joe Mara, to the bank to cash them. When Mara returned, Crater had stuffed papers from his office files into four large portfolios and two briefcases. He told Mara he was going 'up Westchester way for a few days'.

That evening, however, he turned up at his favourite nightclub on 45th Street, but after a few drinks with showgirl Ruby Ritz he left, saying he was going to the theatre.

Amazingly, it was four weeks and a day before the disappearance of one of the city's top judges finally leaked out. Friends and enemies alike, terrified at the idea of a scandal which might implicate them, were desperate to hush up the affair. Manhattan District Attorney, Thomas Crain, was anxious to question Mrs Crater. She refused to talk and the judge's politically-powerful friends kept Crain at bay.

Soon, reports of alleged sightings were coming in from around the world.

In 1955 a photograph of Crater was shown to the Dutch clairvoyant Gerard Croiset. He claimed that the judge had been murdered on the first floor of a farmhouse near the Bronx, New York, and his body buried in the garden.

Remarkably, there was just such a house in the area, which in Crater's day had been used by city officials for secret meetings with their girlfriends. Investigators discovered that the late owner, Henry Krauss, had once claimed that on the morning of 10 August 1930, he had found the kitchen covered with blood ... But of a body there was no sign.

Death at the Opera House

S now swirled silently through the deserted streets and only the footprints of an occasional policeman or passer-by marred its crisp whiteness. It was Christmas in Toronto. But while most people were surrounded by joy, and laughter and goodwill, one woman remained alone, surrounded by silence and suspicion. Three weeks before Christmas Day 1919, Theresa Small's husband had mysteriously disappeared – and there were rumours of murder.

In a few years Ambrose Small, ruthless and mean, had made a fortune out of property. His most important possession was Toronto Grand Opera House. He had started there as an usher. Then he became treasurer. In the end he owned it. He was a millionaire before he was 40 and owned theatres throughout Canada.

At 56 he decided to sell his theatrical empire. A deal was fixed with a financier from Montreal and on 2 December 1919, Small and his wife met him at his lawyers in Toronto. The financier gave Small a cheque for $1,000,000 as down-payment and Small gave the cheque to his wife, who deposited it in his account. The Smalls then went to lunch with their solicitor.

Afterwards Mrs Small went home alone in her chauffeur-driven car while her husband went back to the opera house. He had arranged to meet his solicitor there at 16.00. He was seen entering the theatre. But nobody saw him leave.

His solicitor said later that he had stayed with Small and his secretary, John Doughty, for an hour and a half. Small, he said, was still at the opera house when he left at 17.30.

Doughty left the theatre to have supper with his sister. Later he said he had to go to Montreal and was driven to the station by his sister's husband. On the way they stopped at the opera house, where Doughty collected a small brown paper parcel. He gave this to a second sister in the car and asked her to look after it. Doughty caught the Montreal train – and it was to be two years before he would be back in Toronto.

Small failed to come home that night, so Theresa assumed he had gone to Montreal with Doughty. She waited and waited. But there was no sign of her husband.

It was the opera house manager, however, who raised the alarm. Police issued Small's description – and at once there was a sensational development. Found pinned to the door of a Toronto church was a card which read: 'Prayers for the soul of Ambrose Small.'

The search for a missing man had now become a hunt for a possible murderer. Suspicion fell first on Theresa Small. She was of German extraction, and Germans were far from popular just after World War 1.

Doughty, too, fell under suspicion. But where was he? The police announced rewards of $50,000 for the discovery of Small dead or alive and $15,000 for Doughty.

In the summer of 1920 police obtained a court order to open the strongbox at Small's bank. From their inquiries they expected to find a fortune inside. But bonds worth $105,000 were missing – and the last recorded visitor to Small's safety vaults had been John Doughty. Police investigations intensified. A boilerman at the opera house said that there had been a fight between Small and Doughty on the night Small was last seen alive. Officers raked out the boilers at the opera house looking for human remains.

Then a year later Doughty was discovered working in a lumber camp in Oregon. He was taken back to Toronto and the missing bonds were found in the attic of his sister's house. The police, convinced that they had a murder charge on their hands, confronted Doughty with the alleged fight in the opera house. He vehemently denied it and he was eventually charged with theft.

Doughty said he had taken the bonds from the bank on 2 December to use as a lever against Small who had promised him a share in the theatre deal. But he said he had panicked and fled across the border when he heard of Small's disappearance. Doughty was found guilty of theft and jailed for five years in March 1921.

Yet still there was no sign of Small. Police dug up the floors of his wife's house, but found nothing. Rumours persisted that he had been murdered by racketeers but again widespread searches revealed nothing.

Small was officially declared dead in 1924. Twenty years later the opera house was demolished and detectives made one last effort to solve the case. Again nothing.

To this day what happened to Ambrose Small remains as much a mystery as it was when he vanished off the face of the earth in 1919.

The Impossible *is* Possible

Neither the woman nor her 13-year-old daughter heard the alarm clock ring at 04.00 in the adjoining bedroom. Nor did they hear the soft 'phut' of the silenced gun. If they had, one of America's most baffling murder mysteries might have yielded a clue, however tiny.

Respectable family man Roy Orsini was dead, face-down in his pyjamas, shot in the back of the head by a .38 bullet fired at close range.

On the morning of 12 March 1981, veteran homicide detective Sergeant Tom Farley realized he had the 'impossible' crime on his hands. Orsini had been shot in his bedroom, with the door and windows locked from the inside. He could not possibly have committed suicide.

Orsini, a 38-year-old heating engineer, was a model husband and father. He lived with his wife, Lee, and schoolgirl daughter, Tiffany, in a pleasant suburb at North Little Rock, Arkansas. As far as anyone knew, he hadn't an enemy in the world.

Orsini went to bed early on 11 March to prepare for an early appointment with a client 96 km (60 miles) out of town. He set the alarm for 04.00 to beat the morning traffic jams.

Orsini always slept alone on such nights so that his early rising would not wake the household. The family would sleep in Tiffany's room, next to his own. Soon after 21.00 he kissed them both goodnight and went upstairs to the main bedroom. It was the last time they saw him alive.

Next morning Mrs Orsini rose at 07.00. She and Tiffany had breakfast and walked to the daughter's school nearby. Back home, she began her housework. When her downstairs work finished, she went upstairs to do the bedrooms, starting with her husband's. It was closed, not like Roy at all, she thought. Normally, when he was making an early start, he left the door wide open, and left the room in a bit of a mess.

She tried the handle. The door was locked from the inside. That door had never been locked since they moved in before Tiffany was born 13 years ago. Had he somehow slept in? Had he been taken ill? Again and again, she twisted the handle of the door, knocked and called: 'Roy, Roy, are you all right?'

There was no reply. Lee Orsini, by this time thoroughly alarmed, dashed out of the house and frantically called on next door neighbour Mrs Glenda

Bell. Together the two women managed to prise open the bedroom door. Lee Orsini uttered a piercing scream. Her husband still in his striped pyjamas, lay on the bed.

Sergeant Farley and his squad were on the scene within minutes of receiving Mrs Bell's telephone call. They quickly established that, like many Americans, Roy Orsini had a gun. But it was in a closed drawer several feet from the bed and, although it was a .38, the same calibre as the weapon which had been used to kill him, it was a Smith and Wesson. The fatal bullet had been fired from a Colt. It would anyway have been impossible for Orsini to shoot himself in the back of the head, replace the gun in the drawer and then go back to the bed.

Then there was the problem of the door and windows, all of which had been securely locked from the inside. The alarm clock had been set for 04.00 and had run down. Had the death shot been fired before or after this? There was no means of knowing.

Neither Mrs Orsini nor Tiffany had heard the shot, so the .38 must have been fitted with a silencer.

Farley ordered detailed inquiries into every known relative or business contact of Orsini. A similar discreet check was made on his wife. Both had led totally blameless lives and had been devoted to each other and their daughter. There was nobody who could have had a motive for murder.

Farley said: 'I've been involved with many homicides, but never anything like this. Any way you look at it, it belongs in a book, not in real life.'

A Riddle in Life and a Riddle in Death

One sweltering lunchtime in July, Jimmy Hoffa kissed his wife Josephine, promised to be home by four, and drove away in a bullet-proof limousine.

He was on his way to a lunch date. But how far he got towards keeping his appointment no one knows. For after leaving his luxury home on the outskirts of Detroit at 12.30 on 30 July 1975, Jimmy Hoffa, America's most notorious union boss, was never seen again.

A few hours later an anonymous gravel-voiced phone caller told the police where they could find Hoffa's abandoned car. It sounded more like an

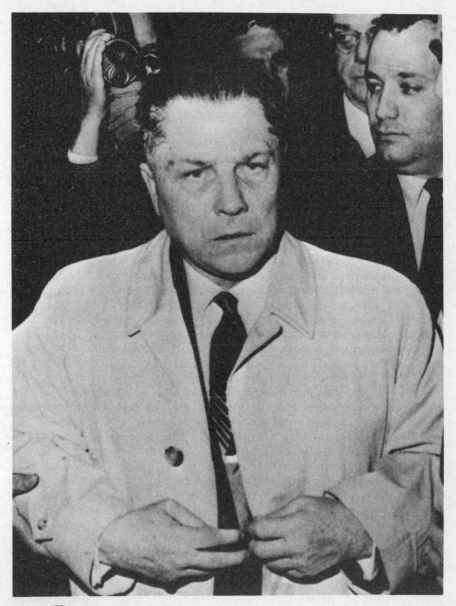

Frank Hoffa

epitaph than a tip-off. They found it shining in the sun, with no sign of a struggle and no body. Just a pair of white gloves neatly folded on the back seat.

There were three main theories about the disappearance of James – middle name Riddle – Hoffa, former president of the Teamsters Union.

The first suggestion was that he was eliminated by the Mafia who feared he would expose illegal 'loans' made by the Teamsters to underworld figures. The second theory was that he died because of a battle for power within the union. The third – and most intriguing – theory was that, knowing there was a contract on his life, he chose to disappear of his own free will. Just two days earlier he had withdrawn more than a million dollars from union funds. Like Hoffa, the money never came back to its rightful home.

His distraught family offered a $200,000 reward for information which might lead to the finding of his body, dead or alive. But there were no takers.

If there were violent and sinister overtones to the disappearance, no one should have been surprised. For this had been the pattern of Hoffa's life almost from the very beginning. As a teenager, he got a job loading trucks and, at 17, he organized his first strike. As a union leader, he favoured lieutenants who had criminal records. Many were chosen for their expertise in terror and extortion. Nevertheless, Hoffa became a hero to many of the Teamsters who had seen their wages virtually doubled in the space of a decade. He also poured millions of dollars into his own pockets and then bought a Miami bank to look after his wealth.

When the crusading Robert Kennedy was made chairman of the Senate Rackets Committee, Hoffa became his prime and very personal target. He described Hoffa's leadership of the Teamsters as a 'conspiracy of evil'. As a result of this probe initiated by Kennedy, Hoffa was eventually jailed in 1967, sentenced to serve 13 years for jury tampering and defrauding the union's pension fund to the tune of almost two million dollars.

Hoffa decreed that Frank Fitzsimmons, a long-time ally, should take his place as president on the strict understanding that he was simply holding down the job until Hoffa regained his freedom.

In 1971, Hoffa was pardoned by President Nixon on condition that he should hold no union office until 1980. But he still had a taste for power, and so began a campaign to persuade the appeal court to lift Nixon's ban.

Fitzsimmons, however, had no intention of relinquishing the reins. Detroit became a battleground as the Fitzsimmons and Hoffa factions fought for supremacy.

This, then, was the background against which Jimmy Hoffa disappeared. It seems probable that the lunch meeting never actually took place. A Hoffa aide received a phone call, supposedly from Hoffa, saying that his companions had not turned up.

But had someone set up the lunch with the intention of luring Hoffa into a trap and then abducting him at gunpoint? This was the theory the FBI favoured.

The FBI also investigated the story of Charles Allen, a former crook turned informer, who became friendly with Hoffa when they were in prison together. Allen claimed that Hoffa was beaten to death by a contract killer known as 'Monster Man' who was 2 m (6 ft 4 in) and weighed 108 kg (17 stone). The body, said Allen, was then taken to New Jersey, cut into small pieces, hidden in two oildrums, and flown to Florida.

The police, unable to verify the story, replaced the Hoffa file in the 'unsolved' category. James Riddle Hoffa was well named.

The Mysterious Mummy

A 'wax' mummy hung in an old amusement park funhouse for 50 years until a strange event revealed its horrible secret – that underneath the ghastly bandages was the embalmed body of an outlaw killed in a turn-of-the-century shootout.

The grim reality surfaced in December 1976, when a television production crew visited the old house to shoot an episode of the TV series *The Six-Million Dollar Man*. Filming was under way when one of the crew gave out a shrill scream ... One of the mummy's stick-like arms had snapped off and fallen. Where it had shattered were leathery shreds of skin and horrible clumps of human tissue clinging to the human bone.

The mummy was rushed to an autopsy room in the Los Angeles county morgue and history's strangest manhunt began. Under the many layers of wax, Los Angeles coroner Dr Thomas Noguchi found the withered body of a man. He had died long ago in his early 30s from a gunshot wound. The corpse had then been carefully embalmed with such heavy concentrations of arsenic that it had turned into a virtual mummy.

The thing had been on display in the Long Beach, California, funhouse since the 1920s, when it was brought from a bankrupt carnival operator. The time lapse meant that the police had little chance of solving the mystery. They feared that the mummy was the victim of a crime. But the only theory that anyone could come up with was stranger even than that. For it was suggested the mummy might have been a criminal himself!

The incredible story put forward by a former employee of the funhouse was that underneath the wax coating was the corpse of an Oklahoma outlaw named Elmer McCurdy.

Oklahoma authorities confirmed that there had been an Elmer McCurdy operating in the wild Oklahoma Territory in the early 1900s. He specialized in robbing trains and banks. After a Jesse James-type robbery in October 1911, McCurdy escaped to an outlaw hangout on the Big Caney River. When a posse from Pawhuska tracked him down, he died in the shootout.

But who would pick up the bill for embalming a footloose outlaw? The undertaker saw only one way to get his money: An embalmed Elmer stood in the corner of the funeral parlour where visitors could gape at him for a nickel apiece. He then fell into the hands of the travelling carnival man who sold him to the amusement park.

Fact or fiction? No one can be sure. The only question worrying Los Angeles county was what to do with the body. The answer was supplied by the Oklahoma Territorial Museum in Guthrie. The outlaw was returned to Oklahoma on 14 April 1977, and in an elegant old hearse pulled by a team of horses, Elmer was buried in the town's Boot Hill cemetery.

The Prairie's Murder Inn

One of the most notorious women in frontier America, bloody Kate Bender, operated a 'murder inn' on the Kansas prairie. Travellers who stopped there for a night were never seen again. For the few dollars in their carpetbags, Kate hid behind a curtain and split the lodger's skulls with a hatchet while they were enjoying one of her home-cooked meals.

Suspicious authorities finally raided the inn, but by that time Kate herself had grown wary. Officials found no trace of the woman, though evidence of her handiwork was plentiful. Digging behind the inn, they unearthed a human boneyard. Few of her victims were identified and the number of dead remains unknown. Even more grisly was the suspicion that Kate had fed some of her victims the flesh of earlier ones.

The riddle of Kate Bender's eerie disappearance intrigued mystery-lovers everywhere. In the hectic little mining camp of Silver City, Idaho, old-timers in the mercantile store pondered it as they sat around the pot-bellied stove.

Kate Bender's home

When Joe Monahan came in for his weekly supplies, they tested their theories on him. Not much of a talker, the young man was always a good listener. When they suggested Kate might have entered a convent or might even be running another murder inn, he simply nodded and went on his way.

To the rest of Silver City, Joe himself was a riddle. A frail little man, he shunned the camp's roaring saloons and girls of the line. Joe's home was a dugout cut into a cliff on Succor Creek near Silver City. To raise the few dollars he spent in the store he kept chickens, pigs and six scrawny cows.

In December 1903, Joe drove his cattle to winter pasture on the Boise River. But the hardships of the trail were too much. Soon after his return to Succor Creek he fell ill and died. When his body was prepared for burial, the barber-mortician ran out of the back room, stunned and sick . . .

Unbelievably, little Joe Monahan had been a woman.

The dugout was ransacked for any clues to her identity. All they found was a yellowed clipping from the *Kansas City Star* about the unsuccessful hunt for Kate Bender. Inevitably, the camp drew its own conclusions: in spite of 'Little Joe's' mild personality, had she been the ruthless killer?

To the day of the funeral there were rumours that a group of 'public minded citizens' meant to dig up the body and send it to Kansas for identification. The minister had heard the rumours too. On that windswept afternoon, he murmured a brief prayer for the unknown woman, then raised his eyes to the graveyard which was jammed with miners. 'I don't believe that this poor woman was a killer,' the minister said. 'Whatever her secret may have been, she died trying to protect it – and, in simple mercy, I ask that you let it die with her.'

The miners drifted away. There was a public subscription that evening in Silver City saloons to cover the burial costs. No one disturbed the unmarked grave. So the mystery lived on.

Who Did She Bury?

In the little coal mining town of McVey, Washington State, Nels Stenstrom and his wife Anna were among the most industrious merchants. Working side by side, they spent twelve hours of almost every day of the week in the McVey Mercantile Store – 'Where Everybody Finds Everything'.

Then a mysterious tragedy entered their lives. On 5 June 1895, Nels Stenstrom vanished without a trace. There were those who said the big man had a roving eye and might possibly have left with a woman. But no one wanted to carry that rumour to the steely-eyed Anna, who was devoted to her husband.

But Anna kept on running the store as if Nels were at her side, and it expanded and grew more prosperous.

In the summer of 1902, Stenstrom was declared legally dead. And that same day Anna made the strange announcement that was to reach newspapers throughout the US: Although he might only be legally dead, she said, he would have a proper grave.

With or without a body, she wanted a casket, a burial plot and fitting church services for her husband.

It was an idea so unusual that crowds of reporters and curious spectators poured into the little town. There was standing room only in the church when the funeral began at 14.30 on 1 July 1902. Nels had been a war veteran, and the vacant coffin was prominently displayed under a US flag. After a few words from the minister, old friends appeared at the lectern to eulogize the departed.

Anna was the last to speak. But she had scarcely started when there was sudden confusion in the crowd. A grizzled derelict in shreds of clothing staggered into an aisle whimpering and clutching his breast. Some said he looked imploringly into Anna's face before he collapsed, unconsious, to the floor.

She was the first to reach him and grope for a pulse. The tears were running down her cheeks when she raised her eyes. All she could say was 'It's Nels.'

The town's one doctor signed the death certificate, marvelling that this alcoholic wreck could be the once powerful Nels. Hundreds watched as the remains of the vagrant were borne to the Stenstrom burial plot.

But the story had an incredible sequel.

While the nearby towns of Roslyn and Cle Elum prospered, the veins of coal ran thin in McVey. It became a shabby ghost town. After Anna died and was buried with her husband, a contractor bought the store for its old lumber.

When he was bulldozing the building down, shallow graves were found beneath the floorboards. Two skeletons lay side by side. Between them was the axe that had split their skulls.

One was the skeleton of a woman destined to remain as nameless as the vagrant buried with Anna. The man's body was equally unidentifiable ... Could it have been the body of the real Nels Stenstrom?

Acrobats of Death

U go Pavesi stepped out onto the third-storey balcony of his home. An extortionist and general hoodlum, he liked to spend his evenings there while he plotted further criminal enterprises.

Usually, he would have been accompanied by his girlfriend but on this occasion 17-year-old Lorna Perricone was in hospital. As a disciplinary measure, he had put her there himself with a dozen savage blows to the face and stomach.

In the street below Pavesi's home, there were three witnesses who later reported seeing an impossible sight. They claimed to have seen a black giant 5.4 m (18 ft) tall emerge from the shadows and make his way towards the man on the balcony. The giant lifted him casually from the deck chair and let his squat body plunge to the pavement. Pavesi's severed head fell beside it, wrung from the body in an incredible display of strength.

In the deep, soft soil of the shrubbery surrounding Pavesi's home, police found the footprints of the killer. Displacement of the soil indicated that he had weighed no less than 410 kg (900 lb). But he had vanished completely in the confusion that followed the murder at Van Nuys, California, on the night of 13 November 1941, and no one knew where he would strike again.

A shrewd policeman who had been only a few blocks from the area was put on the case. Sergeant Lou Grandin toured the run-down area. One of his calls was on a psychic who called herself Madame Olga.

His visit was interrupted by the entrance of the old lady's three boarders, the powerful Perricone brothers Mario, Tony and Giorgio. Big, balding men with no-nonsense eyes, their timing and precision as an acrobatic team had won them high praise.

Mario, the spokesman, told Grandin that in 50 years of theatrical experience he had never known a giant like the alleged Van Nuys killer. Then he shocked the policeman by telling him: 'The girl Pavesi put in hospital was our sister, sergeant. And I'm using the past tense because she died a few minutes ago.'

'I'm sorry,' Grandin said humbly. 'I ask only that you stay in San Francisco until we get this thing cleaned up.'

But it was a warning that went unheeded. The date was 7 December, 1941 and something was to happen that day that changed the history of the world. The Perricone brothers were among the first to enlist after Pearl Harbor. So, too, was Sergeant Lou Grandin.

The case of the vanishing giant preyed on Grandin's mind throughout the war. On his return to the United States, he decided to pay one last visit to Madame Olga. The aged psychic was still alive but frail.

She told the ex-cop that the Perricone brothers had all died in the war – which was why she felt free to suggest a possible explanation for the death of Ugo Pavesi.

She drew out a yellowed vaudeville poster. There were the three Perricone brothers in the centre of the stage, Mario with Tony standing proudly on his shoulders. And on Tony's shoulders stood Giorgio, ripping a thick telephone directory to shreds in his big hands. The three would have made an impressive giant: Mario the planner, Tony the middleman, and Giorgio – with the huge, powerful hands.

The Oldest Kidnap Victim?

Excited scientists named him Peking Man. He was a collection of bones about 500,000 years old, unearthed near Peking in the 1920s and a vital missing link in man's knowledge of evolution. Then, in 1941, with the Japanese advancing on the city it was decided to ship the bones to America – they still have not arrived.

Dr Harry L Shapiro, former Professor of Anthropology at Columbia University, has been searching for them ever since. His theory is that they were purloined by a Marine officer who took Peking man back to America.

The story was given credence when a Chicago businessman offered $5,000 to anybody with information. A mysterious woman met the businessman on the 102nd floor of the Empire State Building in New York. She said that her husband had returned from China with fossils of some prehistoric man. She produced a photograph of the remains but before a deal could be made the woman disappeared without trace.

The FBI have followed reports of GIs returning home from Asia with strange-looking skulls, as souvenirs – without success.

A Sydney businessman maintained he had acquired the bones and buried them in a forest in Tasmania. He would reveal the spot at a price.

It is possible that Peking Man is now in both America and Australia or even in Britain. The mystery of this strange kidnap remains unsolved.

Chapter
Five

Murder
Most Foul

House of Horror

When Timothy Evans walked into the police station at Merthyr Tydfil, South Wales, he was distressed and confused. He told the desk sergeant: 'I want to give myself up. I have disposed of the body of my wife.'

Evans went on to explain that he was spending a lonely self-imposed exile in Wales with relatives and that the body of his dead wife would be found in a drain at their home in London, at 10 Rillington Place, Notting Hill, where Evans rented the top floor flat.

The first police search on 30 November 1949, produced nothing. But Evans, a 24-year-old semi-literate van driver insisted that his wife was dead, the result of an attempted abortion carried out by their downstairs neighbour John Reginald Halliday Christie.

A fresh search by police produced evidence of a grisly double murder. In a small back-yard wash-house they found the body of Beryl Evans. And they found a dead baby, Evan's daughter Geraldine.

Evans seemed shattered by his daughter's death but quietly and morosely, confessed to both murders. At his trial a few months later, he retracted his admissions and blamed Christie for their murders. His accusations against his respectable neighbour hardly carried any weight in court.

Christie, aged 55, was a diligent Post Office Savings Bank clerk who had done his duty as a reserve Metropolitan policeman a few years earlier during World War 2.

Evans tried to claim in court that Christie, who often pretended to have some medical knowledge, had bungled an abortion on Beryl and she had died. Confused and hesitant, Evans insisted that Christie had promised that he would dispose of Beryl's body down the drain and arrange for baby Geraldine to be cared for by a young couple who lived nearby. Evans had given up his job and left the baby behind for 'adoption', going off to live in Wales until he could bear his guilty secret no longer. Under cross-examination he floundered deeper and deeper into hopeless excuses about why he had confessed to the murders and then turned his story round to implicate his neighbour.

Reginald Christie, who had lived quietly at Rillington Place for a dozen years with his wife Ethel, gave his evidence with calm assurance and heard the prosecution describe him as 'this perfectly innocent man'.

That was enough for the jury. They found Timothy Evans guilty of the

10 Rillington Place

murder of baby Geraldine and had no need to proceed on the charge of the murder of Beryl.

Evans was hanged and the murders dismissed as a squalid tragic case of a rather stupid young man who had cracked under the pressure of living in the London slums, earning a pittance and trying to support his family. That, it appeared at the time, was all there was to it.

What the jury and the police did not know was that 10 Rillington Place was not just the temporary crypt of Beryl and Geraldine Evans. The nondescript terrace house was a veritable graveyard. And Reginald Christie was far from the pompous, respectable minor civil servant he pretended to be.

When the police began their first search for the body of Beryl Evans, they had literally been standing on top of the bodies of the previous victims of Christie's bizarre sexual killings.

As the detectives had surveyed Christie's barren patch of back garden, discussing the possibility of digging there, Christie's little mongrel dog began scratching the soil and pawing at the skull of one of the two women he had already murdered, Muriel Eady. Christie shooed the dog away and casually kicked the earth back into place.

The police decided to have another pry around the drains and outbuildings. When they found bodies in the wash-house they were satisfied. Christie, close to panic, unearthed the skull that night and hurried off across Notting Hill with it tucked under his raincoat. He threw it into the remains of a gutted building where it was found next day by two schoolboys. And Muriel Eady was duly logged by police as an unidentified and previously undiscovered victim of the wartime bombing blitz.

Christie had a close call when the police came to investigate the deaths of Beryl and Geraldine Evans. But as the nervous shock subsided, his lust to kill again overcame his fear.

Christie's wife Ethel had no reason to suspect that two murder victims were already buried in the garden. But she may have thought that her husband was more involved in the deaths of Beryl and Geraldine than he admitted to her. She was silenced anyway by Christie, strangled and her body hidden beneath the boards of the sitting-room floor. In quick succession Christie lured three more women to his flat, all prostitutes, and killed them. It was said he could only gain sexual satisfaction from dead women.

With the remains of six dead bodies buried in the garden, dumped into a crudely papered-over kitchen cupboard and hunched underneath the floorboards, Christie left Rillington Place and moved to other lodgings.

On 24 March 1953, a prospective new tenant looking over the flat detected a foul smell from the sealed kitchen cupboard. He picked away at the wallpaper until he could glance inside – and then went straight to the police.

They arrested Reginald Christie and then began the long re-investigation into the guilt or innocence of Timothy Evans who had been hanged three years earlier.

The wave of public outrage over the murders and the execution of Evans provoked a stormy debate in Parliament and led to the suspension of capital punishment for a period of five years. But not before Reginald Christie was convicted, sentenced and hanged for murder.

Christie had hoped to cheat the noose by confessing gleefully to mass murder and having the jury judge him insane. 'The more the merrier', he confessed.

He outlined his bizarre method of killing his victims – first getting them drunk, then forcing them to inhale coal gas from the mains supply until they were unconscious. He then strangled and raped them.

Christie confessed to murdering Beryl Evans, although strangely, he denied killing baby Geraldine – a murder that Timothy Evans had already confessed to after admitting to the murder of his wife.

John Reginald Halliday Christie

Was it possible that two men, both strangers and both unaware of each other's murderous characters, had lived together under the same roof? Such a coincidence seemed unbelievable.

In 1966 a judicial review of the case under Mr Justice Brabin concluded it more probable that Evans murdered his own wife but not his baby daughter.

No one knows for sure who killed Beryl Evans. Her husband Timothy and Reginald Christie both took their terrible secrets to the gallows with them. Only one of the two men knew the complete certainty whether or not the other one was lying.

Poetry, Passion and Prison

Adelaide Bartlett was boyishly attractive, with bobbed hair, full lips and flashing eyes. She had few friends outside her husband's immediate family, and even they were often at loggerheads with the wilful young foreigner who had come into their midst.

Adelaide was born in Orléans, France, in 1856 to an English father and a wealthy, but unmarried, French mother. At the age of 17 she came to England to complete her education, staying in London at the home of her guardian. A regular visitor to the house was her guardian's brother, Edwin Bartlett, who speedily wooed, won and wed her.

Edwin, who at 29 was 10 years older than Adelaide, was a hard working and prosperous family grocer, a kindly man – but one whose life-style was not to his young bride's taste.

Adelaide fell out with Edwin's family – all except his younger brother, Frederick, with whom she had an affair. While Edwin devoted himself ever more diligently to his business, the bored wife remained at home sewing and organizing the household chores – and waiting for Frederick's illicit visits.

She made so little secret of her attraction to Frederick that the brothers' father intervened. After one acrimonious row, during which Adelaide learned that the older Mr Bartlett was planning to move in to the family home at her husband's invitation, she stormed from the house and was not seen again for some days. Since Frederick was also absent for this period, tongues began to wag ... so much so that when Adelaide's anger cooled and she returned home, she forced her father-in-law to write a letter of apology to her.

In 1885 the Bartletts moved to a grander home in Pimlico. There they were visited regularly by a young Wesleyan minister with a penchant for poetry, the Rev. George Dyson.

Edwin considered Dyson to be an improving influence on his wife and encouraged their friendship. What he may not have realized was that the minister's flowery poetry was often directed at Adelaide. He wrote to her:

Who is it that hath burst the door,
Unclosed the heart that shut before
And set her queen-like on its throne
And made its homage all her own?
My Birdie!

The Rev. Dyson did not confine his expressions of love to the written word. And his love affair with Adelaide was aided by her husband's strange reaction to the couple's growing closeness. Bartlett not only condoned his wife's friendship, he actively encouraged it. He even made a will leaving everything to his wife and naming Dyson as the executor.

Then, in December 1885, Edwin Bartlett fell ill. He had always prided himself on being particularly fit but this illness, diagnosed by the family

The trial of Adelaide Bartlett

doctor as acute gastritis, took its toll on him and he sank fast. Edwin died on New Year's Day 1886.

The doctor was sufficiently suspicious to press for a post-mortem examination, which revealed large quantities of liquid chloroform in his stomach. Everything pointed to poisoning. Yet there was one inexplicable fact ... there were no traces of the burning chloroform in Edwin's mouth or throat.

Both lovers were charged with murder, although the case against Dyson was later dropped for lack of evidence despite his admission that he had bought quantities of chloroform at various chemists' shops.

At her trial, the attractive Adelaide played brilliantly on the emotions and Victorian prejudices of the jury. She admitted dosing her husband with chloroform. But she claimed pathetically that she had first used the drug to curb his sexual demands, then later to help Edwin sleep during his illness.

The jury were sympathetic. They were also baffled by the means by which the chloroform was administered without causing burning of the throat. They acquitted Adelaide Bartlett, who disappeared without trace after her trial. It was reported that she had emigrated to America.

A famous surgeon, Sir James Paget of London's St Bartholomew's Hospital, commented: 'Now that it is all over, she should tell us in the interests of science how she did it.'

The Vicar and the Choirmistress

Even today the headlines would cause a sensation ... 'Vicar And Choirmistress Murdered In Lovers' Lane'. The congregation were scandalized to learn of the a love affair between their clergyman and a married woman and horrified by the killing. Yet no one was ever convicted of the double murder, and the mystery remains to this day.

A courting couple discovered the bodies of the Rev. Edward Wheeler Hall and Mrs Eleanor Mills, choir leader at his church, on 16 September 1922. The spot, by an abandoned farm near New Brunswick, New Jersey, was a favourite with lovers seeking solitude.

Hall, minister of St John the Evangelist Church, in New Brunswick, and his mistress had both been shot through the head. But more sinister ... the choir leader's vocal cords had been cut in an act of savage hate. The pair's passionate letters to each other were strewn contemptuously around the bodies.

Hall's wife Frances was questioned, as was Mrs Mills' husband James, but no charges were brought. Mrs Hall was a popular figure among the church-going community. There were stories of detectives ignoring clues, of vital evidence going missing, and of a prosecutor unwilling to take action. There was neither a post-mortem nor an inquest.

There the case might have been conveniently closed, but for a news-hungry editor convinced there had been a cover-up.

Philip Payne of the *New York Mirror*, sent his own sleuths to the scene to piece together the evidence. They managed to get hold of Hall's calling card, which police had found propped against his body, and Payne claimed it carried the fingerprints of Mrs Hall's brother Willie.

Faced with this and other evidence, police brought murder charges against Mrs Hall, her cousin Henry Carpender, a brother Henry Stevens and Willie.

Willie, the strangest defendant, was an eccentric who liked to dress up in fireman's uniform and put out fires in his own backyard.

They were finally brought to trial four years after the killings, in November 1926. After so long, memories were failing. The wealthy Mrs Hall's high-powered lawyers made mincemeat of the prosecution witnesses' shaky testimony.

Soon it became clear that the prosecution's case rested on one alleged eye-witness – Jane Gibson, a pig farmer. Dying of cancer, she was wheeled into court in a hospital bed and whispered her vital evidence.

Four years earlier, then a fit and vigorous countrywoman, she said she had been exercising her mule Jennie on the night of the murders. She identified the four defendants and said she had seen them in the lane where the bodies were later found.

With them were the Rev. Hall and Mrs Mills. Voices were raised in anger, she said and there was mention of love letters. Mrs Gibson rode away, wanting no part of a family quarrel.

Her testimony, delivered firmly despite her pain, obviously impressed the jury. But then a relative gave evidence denying that Mrs Gibson had been out of the house that night.

Moments later the courtroom was rocked by the news that a prisoner in jail in New York had confessed to the killings. But he was exposed as a sensation-seeker who was nowhere near New Brunswick when the murders were comitted.

Witnesses gave the Stevens brothers and cousin Henry watertight alibis, and the defence then suggested that Mrs Gibson had shot the couple, thinking they were thieves after her corn.

But the most telling witness of all was the incredibly calm Mrs Hall. She had loved her husband dearly, she said, and had never suspected an infidelity. Least of all with Eleanor Mills, whom she had always regarded as her dearest friend.

Mrs Hall said she could not account for Jane Gibson's testimony, but would forgive her because of her suffering. The jury believed the wronged wife, and all four defendants were acquitted.

It was a subdued crowd who left the courtroom, knowing that somewhere in their midst a killer was still at large.

And some strange events followed.

Mrs Hall sued the *New York Mirror* for two million dollars.

Philip Payne, desperate to rebuild his reputation, set out to make a record transatlantic flight to Rome. His plane vanished.

Officials who had been accused of concealing evidence lived under a cloud. And those involved in the prosecution were eased from office.

Witnesses for both sides were struck by a succession of tragedies. Soon after Mrs Gibson's death, Mrs Hall also died of cancer. And so, one by one, did the other defendants.

The case remains unsolved.

Death in Happy Valley

When 57-year-old Sir Henry 'Jock' Delves Broughton married a young blonde with a passion for clothes and jewels in 1940, he told her: 'If you ever fall in love with someone else and want a divorce, I won't stand in your way.'

The old Etonian baronet also promised his beautiful bride Diana, 30 years his junior, an income of £5,000 a year for 7 years should she ever leave him for another man.

Just three months after the marriage, Diana did exactly that. She fell in love with another Old Etonian, Josslyn Hay, the 39-year-old Earl of Erroll.

The brevity of the marriage would seem extraordinary even in more modern, permissive times. But in the strange, close circle in which Hay and

Above: Josslyn Hay's car
Right: Josslyn Hay

the Broughtons lived, it was not too unorthodox. Their home was an area of colonial Kenya known as Happy Valley, where wild drinking, cocaine-snorting and wife-swapping were prevalent in 1940.

Josslyn Hay himself was a dedicated philanderer whose favourite saying was 'to hell with husbands'. But his amoral attitude appeared not to worry Sir Henry, the cuckolded husband. At a dinner party he threw at the local country club, he toasted his wife and her lover: 'I wish them every happiness and may their union be blessed with an heir. To Diana and Joss.'

Broughton returned home visibly drunk, leaving Erroll and Diana to dance. Erroll then drove off alone, remarking as he left: 'The old boy's so nice, it smells bad.'

Two hours later Erroll was found on the floor of his Buick, a bullet through his head. But the murder weapon was not to be seen.

Though Broughton seemed the obvious suspect, such was the cuckolded baronet's calm and masterful conduct in the witness box that he was found 'not guilty'.

After the acquittal Broughton and Diana soon split up. He committed suicide the following year, still protesting his innocence.

Lizzie and the Axe

Crime historians still work to clear the name of Lizzie Borden, long portrayed as the fiendish axe-murderer who 'gave her mother 40 whacks . . . and her father 41.'

Although Hollywood labelled poor Lizzie a killer and gossips insisted she was a cruel murderess, the 32-year-old spinster was actually acquitted by a jury and lived to a ripe old age, a gentle woman and a benefactor to animals. But until her death in 1937, she was taunted by one of the most cruel jingles in history:

Lizzie Borden took an axe
And gave her mother 40 whacks
When she saw what she had done
She gave her father 41.

In a popular television movie actress Elizabeth Montgomery portrayed Lizzie as a vicious killer who hacked her parents to death in the nude to avoid getting bloodstains on her dress. But many people believe that Lizzie was really the victim of bungling officials who let the real killer slip through their fingers.

Her ordeal began on the morning of 4 August 1892. In the living room of a bleak old house in Fall River, Massachusetts, Lizzie found her father, banker Andrew Borden with his head beaten to 'an unrecognizable pulp'. He lay on a blood-soaked sofa, where he had apparently been napping when the murderer struck. And in the horror of that discovery it would be an hour before Lizzie knew that there were other horrors ahead.

The young woman's stepmother, Abby Borden, had supposedly been called from the house to the sickbed of a friend. But she had not gone after all. She was on the floor of an upstairs guest room, her skull a mass of blood and splintered bone.

Inescapably, the net began to tighten around Lizzie Borden. She told police she had been in the barn looking for fish-line sinkers when the killings took place.

Bridget Sullivan, the Borden's hired girl had been upstairs dozing through the heat of the day. Emma Borden, Lizzie's older sister had been out of town. And John V. Morse, a visiting uncle, had been out making business calls. Excluding Bridget – whom Lizzie 'vouched for' – that left Lizzie herself.

Lizzie Borden was brought to trial in June 1893 and the evidence at first began to stack against her. There had been no love lost between the Borden daughters and their shrewish stepmother, who reputedly nagged at her husband to cut them off without a penny. Nor had there been any show of affection for their father, whose stinginess and domestic tyranny were bywords in Fall River.

It was suggested that Lizzie had butchered her parents in an epileptic seizure and had no memories of the crime. But police had unearthed no murder weapon, no witnesses, no shreds of bloody clothing, and the circumstantial evidence was just too flimsy.

Acquitted to a chorus of rousing cheers, Lizzie went back to the bleak old house. She was to share with her sister until 1923, when they parted company.

There were suspicions about three people who had testified against Lizzie but, for reasons never explained, the police failed to reopen the case.

As the years passed, the old jingle haunted Lizzie Borden's life and wax museums continued to cast her as an axe-wielding fiend. Friends deserted her. In her last days, there were no visitors in the Fall River house. She died leaving a fortune to charity, including a $30,000 bequest to the Society for the Prevention of Cruelty to Animals. Gentle in life and forgiving in death, she said nothing about the agonies she had once suffered.

The Harry Oakes Affair

The sub-tropical paradise of the Bahamas boasts 700 islands and rocky islets or cays, most of them uninhabited, surrounded by the sparkling blue-green waters of the Gulf Stream. Only 80 km (50 miles) away across the horizon is the millionaire's paradise of Miami and all the brash excitement of Florida, Land of the Stars and Stripes.

The Union Jack flies in Nassau, capital of the Bahamas, testimony to its position as an outpost of British civilization and administration, a veneer of respectability over its fabled history as a haven for buccaneers and rum runners, adventures and soldiers of fortune.

But to Edward Albert Patrick David, Duke of Windsor, former monarch of the British Empire, life in the Bahamas had held all the appeal of exile in an Arctic waste. His appointment as Governor General in August 1940 was seen as a deliberate punishment by the wartime cabinet of Winston Churchill.

For four years, since his abdication as King Edward VIII, the headstrong and impetuous duke had been a grave embarassment to his government and loyal subjects. He had provoked a constitutional crisis and world-wide scandal when he abdicated his throne to marry the woman he loved, American divorcee Wallis Simpson. A year after their marriage the duke and his restless American duchess had even visited Nazi Chancellor Adolf Hitler in Germany while he was arming his nation for war against Britain. The duke quickly became a propaganda pawn for the Nazis.

The duke had only set foot on English soil once since his marriage before being caught up in the roaring tide of war as the Germans invaded France and sped towards the Windsors' new adopted home in Paris.

The former king and his wife fled south to neutral Spain and sought safety in Madrid. Fearful that the duke might be the victim of a kidnap and used as a hostage, Churchill asked him to return home by flying boat to Britain.

But the Duke of Windsor, resentful that his wife would not be accorded any privilege or status as a member of the royal family, refused. He chose the only alternative Churchill gave him, the post of Governor General of the Bahamas, thousands of miles across the Atlantic where he could be safely isolated from the intrigues of wartime Europe.

Lonely and ostracized, the Windsors arrived in Nassau to be greeted by the Bahamas' most prominent citizen, Sir Harry Oakes. Sir Harry's title was no genteel hereditary honour from a long line of ennobled forefathers. He was reputedly one of the richest men in the Empire, a newly created baronet, a self-made multi-millionaire. He was a ruthless businessman who had battled and bullied his way to the top from a hell-raising existence as a Yukon and Alaskan gold prospector. This hardened man of the world swiftly became the Duke of Windsor's close friend.

Their social and personal lives became entwined and Oakes even turned over his palatial home in Nassau to the Windsors while the Governor General's mansion was refurbished. The two men were constant drinking and dining companions on their frequent trips to the American mainland where Oakes introduced the duke to his social and business acquaintances.

The duke's lifetime of royal grooming as a man born to handle the gravest of personal and national crises helped him maintain his composure on the morning of 8 July 1943 when his equerry roused him from sleep and told him that Oakes was dead. He had been savagely beaten and stabbed, his skull had been fractured and an attempt had been made to burn his bloodstained body beyond recognition.

The former king quickly invoked his authority under the Emergency War Powers Act, using his powers of censorship to insist that news of Sir Harry's murder should be hushed up. A few hours later he belatedly put the wheels of legal investigation into motion – by calling in a personal contact in the Miami police.

The duke made the baffling request to Miami Police Department: 'I think one of our leading citizens has committed suicide. Can you come and confirm this?' In fact Sir Harry Oakes's 'suicide' had all the hallmarks of a Mafia gangland contract killing.

Harry Oakes had not been born a British subject. The son of a schoolteacher in Sangerville, Maine, he was a daydreamer who spent his college days boasting of the great fortune he planned to amass. After two years as a student doctor at Syracuse he gave up college. Harry told his fellow students, all dedicated young medical men: 'You can make a good living, but you'll never get filthy rich as a doctor. I want to be filthy rich.'

Harry put his medical training to use as a hospital orderly in the prospecting camps of the Canadian north, treating frostbite and gangrene and malnutrition, while he gleaned every scrap of information he could from experienced old panhandlers.

For 14 years he followed the restless waves of prospectors chasing every elusive strike from California to Yukon, Australia and the Congo. His dogged persistence paid off in 1910 when, with a partner, he finally struck gold at Kirkland Lake in northern Ontario. It was the second largest gold find in North America and over the next 12 years he connived and wheedled and spent part of his growing fortune to buy out his partner's interests and gain sole control.

Oakes was a crude and ruthless tycoon by 1923 when, at the age of 48, he married Australian bank typist Eunice MacIntyre who he met on a cruise liner. To strengthen his links with the country which provided his massive wealth, Oakes renounced his American citizenship and became a naturalized Canadian.

But Harry Oakes became disenchanted with his adopted country as his tax bill climbed higher and higher and he found himself paying 85 per cent of his income to the taxman.

On holiday with his wife and five children at one of his homes in Palm Beach, he met real estate promoter Harold Christie who boasted of the tax advantages of the Bahamas, where the British administration charged no income tax or death duties. It did not take Oakes long to decide to protect his fortune by moving to Nassau and he became a grateful benefactor. He poured millions of pounds into the islands, buying hotels and landscaping golf courses, funding charities to provide milk for children and hospitals for the poor.

His generosity soon spilled over into Britain itself where he bestowed £250,000 on one hospital. A grateful King George VI, the Duke of Windsor's younger brother who had succeeded to the throne after the Abdication, conferred a baronetcy on him in 1939.

The colourful and brash businessman who greeted the Windsors on their arrival set about making himself the power behind the Duke of Windsor's new 'throne'. All major legislation required the consent of the Governor General – the duke – and Sir Harry had him eating out of his hand.

This was the cosy relationship that real estate developer Harold Christie had to explain to his business associate when they met in Palm Beach, Florida, to discuss the prospect of opening a casino in the Bahamas.

He had already ingratiated himself with the duke and had his tacit endorsement. But Sir Harry was blowing hot and cold about the plan. Harold Christie may have wanted to apply some more gentle persuasion to the cantankerous old tycoon when he met him on the night of 7 July 1943 at Sir Harry's palatial home 'Westbourne' in Nassau.

Sir Harry was due to leave in two days time to join his family at yet another holiday home, in Maine, and Christie could not afford to miss the opportunity for some business talk. Sir Harry had guests to a small dinner party that night but they left at 23.00.

Then, according to Harold Christie, he went to bed and Christie retired to another bedroom further down the corridor. Neither man left the house again that night, Christie claimed, and although wakened during the night by the thunder of a tropical storm, he heard no sound from Sir Harry's bedroom.

When he rose for breakfast at 07.00 he strolled along the balcony to the screen door leading to the master bedroom and called out for Sir Harry. There was no reply, so he waited a few seconds and stepped inside.

Christie chilled at the sight that greeted him. The room was filled with smoke, but there was no fire. Sir Harry Oakes lay on his back on the bed, his face caked with blood, his skull fractured with four puncture marks, his flimsy pyjamas burned off and sticking to the open blisters on his charred skin.

Christie's calls of alarm alerted a housekeeper and within minutes he made the first of his frantic telephone calls to the Island Police Commissioner and to the Governor General, the Duke of Windsor.

The Bahamas police were no experts in matters of sudden, violent death and it was not entirely without relief that the commissioner received the news that the duke had asked for help from the Miami Police Department to confirm Sir Harry's 'suicide'.

The duke had spoken to Captain Edward Melchen, chief of the homicide bureau, a policeman who was also a personal friend, having acted as a bodyguard for the duke on his frequent visits to Miami. Within hours, Melchen arrived in Nassau accompanied by another trusted detective, Captain James Barker. The two men made one cursory inspection of the blistered body on the smoke-blackened bed.

'Face up to it,' Melchen told the Duke. 'This is no suicide.'

Throughout the following day, while the two Americans set up a temporary headquarters at 'Westbourne' interviewing members of the staff and the dead baronet's family, Christie and the Duke of Windsor kept in constant touch with each other by telephone. That afternoon the duke visited the murder house himself to see the scene of the gruesome crime and he spent some twenty minutes alone with Captain James Barker.

Two hours later, a suspect for the murder of Sir Harry Oakes was arrested.

Alfred de Marigny was a lean, lanky 36-year-old with a dark complexion, a native of the Indian Ocean island of Mauritius. He was also Sir Harry Oakes's son-in-law.

De Marigny had been married and divorced twice before he began his courtship of 17-year-old Nancy, Sir Harry's eldest daughter. He had been living in the Bahamas squandering the divorce settlement from his wealthy second wife when he set his sights on Nancy, and the locals all agreed he was a shiftless gigolo.

His relationship with his mercurial father-in-law had been stormy ever since de Marigny's marriage to Nancy in New York two days after her 18th birthday ... two days after becoming old enough to marry without her parents' consent.

At the time of her father's death, Nancy de Marigny had been in Florida for medical treatment and Alfred had thrown a dinner party with his houseguest and 'hanger-on', fellow Mauritian playboy George de Videlou.

Alfred left the house at 01.00 to drive two of his guests home. His route could have taken him past 'Westbourne' in the middle of the night, the prosecution insisted at his trial.

And there was evidence to link him with the murder, prosecuting attorney Eric Hallinan claimed. Whoever killed Sir Harry tried to spread flames around the room to burn evidence of the crime. And when de Marigny was examined by police, it was found the hairs on his right arm had been singed and burned.

More importantly, according to the prosecution de Marigny's fingerprints was found on an ornamental Chinese screen in the murder bedroom.

The importance of the singed hairs on de Marigny's arms was quickly squashed by defence counsel Godfrey Higgs who extracted testimony from a witness, one of de Marigny's dinner guests, that Sir Harry's son-in-law had scorched his arm trying to light a candle inside a lantern on the dinner table.

The evidence of the fingerprint became the crucial turning point in the case and highlighted some inexplicably inept investigation. Miami cop Captain James Barker testified that he had 'lifted' a fingerprint of Alfred de Marigny from the Chinese screen. He had used a gummed strip of rubber to obtain the imprint of the moist fingermark – at the same time destroying any permanent evidence that the print had been on the surface of the screen.

The space where de Marigny's print was alleged to have been was blank. Captain Barker, whose evidence became more hesitant, admitted he had not brought his own camera with him from Miami to photograph fingerprint evidence 'in situ'. He told the court, quite reasonably: 'I thought I was coming to confirm a suicide. The fingerprint camera didn't seem important.'

Barker's credibility was finally demolished by the defence's own expert, Maurice O'Neil of the New Orleans Police Department, a past president of the International Association of Identification. He examined a photograph of the sharp contours of de Marigny's fingerprint and declared it could not have been lifted off the screen without being superimposed on the pattern of intricate etchings which also covered the screen.

De Marigny's fingerprint, he deduced, had been lifted from a smooth surface, possibly from a tumbler or a cigarette packet the accused man had handled in Sir Harry's bedroom long after the murder when he was invited to the house by the American detectives.

Defence attorney Higgs never made any suggestion why he thought Captain Barker should give such blatantly phoney evidence. And there was little explanation for another crucial piece of cross examination . . .

Harold Christie, the property developer who slept in the murder house, swore on oath that neither he nor Sir Harry had left 'Westbourne' after 23.00

that night. Then Higgs called to the witness stand Captain Edward Sears, a reliable Bahamian policeman, assistant superintendent in charge of traffic.

Sears, who had know Christie since their schooldays together, confidently testified that he had seen him in George Street, Nassau, at 01.00 on the night of the murder. Christie had been a passenger in a station wagon speeding away from the direction of Nassau harbour. Sears could not identify the other man in the car, the driver. He only knew he was a white man, a stranger to the islands.

The jury retired for two hours to consider their verdict. They found Alfred de Marigny not guilty of the murder of his father-in-law.

No one else was ever charged with the murder of Sir Harry Oakes.

One blood-spattered clue to the identity of the man who may have murdered Sir Harry was uncovered nearly ten years later in Miami, on 26 December 1952, when Captain James Barker was killed by a .38 bullet from his own revolver.

The trigger was pulled by his son who tearfully told Dade County Court that Captain Barker had become a violent drug addict, corrupt and depraved. The policeman's slaying at the hands of his son was ruled 'justifiable homicide'.

It came as no surprise to his colleagues who had known for years that Barker was on the payroll of Meyer Lansky, the tough and ruthless gangster who ran the Mafia crime syndicate in Florida and Cuba.

At the time of Sir Harry's death, Lansky desperately wanted official approval to open a lucrative gambling casino in Nassau. He pulled every trick he knew and used the services of any influential people in the Bahamas he thought could be won over to his cause.

Lansky told his henchmen that one obstinate man was standing in his path and would have to be taught a lesson.

To this day people in the Bahamas still talk about the powerful motor cruisers which used to slip in and out of Nassau harbour any time they pleased, without bothering with customs and immigration formalities. They were the ships of Lansky's fleet, crewed by gun-toting skippers who knew the waters between Miami and Nassau from the days of Prohibition, when they ran illicit booze from the liquor warehouses of the British Bahamas to the speakeasies of Florida.

If Harold Christie was seen sitting as a terrified passenger in a car speeding from the docks the night Sir Harry Oakes was murdered, had he been to a meeting aboard one of those boats? Had Sir Harry been with him?

Was Sir Harry's bleeding body hunched in the back of the station wagon, fatally beaten after telling Lansky's emissaries that nobody pushed Harry Oakes around, not even the Mob?

The unidentified white man seen by police Superintendent Sears ... was the man Meyer Lansky sent to Nassau to teach Sir Harry Oakes a lesson?

Did Captain James Barker, the Miami policeman on Lansky's payroll, have orders to find a scapegoat? Did he try to frame the hapless de Marigny to shift suspicion from a contract killer?

As soon as decently possible after the end of World War 2 the Duke of Windsor left the Bahamas, hurrying back to a civilized European exile in Paris. He never discussed the Oakes murder.

Harold Christie was later knighted for his services to the Government of the Bahamas. He died in September 1973 while travelling in Germany.

Killings in the Congo

Assassination is the murder which touches the lives of millions and changes the course of history. The life of a national hero is ended by a bullet from a telescopic rifle, or a tyrant and his entourage are swept away in one blast from a hidden bomb.

The motives of a single assassin can be complex, from a madman harbouring a murderous grudge for some imagined injustice, to a lone patriot willing to sacrifice his own life to end the rule of a dictator. Often assassination is murder by committee, by a political group who want to wrest power from their opponents by destroying their figurehead.

Almost always assassination is an open outrage. The murder of a public figure usually has to be carried out in a public place, a factor dictated by the need to catch the victim when he is most exposed and vulnerable – and often a grisly ploy by the assassins to demonstrate their power and determination before a stunned audience. Assassins plot murder in secret and kill in public. And they are not slow to accept the responsibility for their crime. The lone madman is rewarded with the public platform he seeks, the political committee want to announce their success widely and clearly.

But the deaths of two prominent political figures within nine months of each other in 1961 may have provided rare case histories of assassinations unadmitted and undeclared.

Both deaths are linked together in the turbulent world of African politics. One was explained away as an unplanned, unfortunate killing. The other was

Patrice Lumumba shows his wrist which was injured during imprisonment

neatly catalogued as a fatal flying accident, the understandable failure of man and machine on a tricky night flight. Doubts still linger about the real causes of the deaths of firebrand African revolutionary Patrice Lumumba and international statesman Dag Hammarskjoeld, the peace-making Secretary General of the United Nations.

Patrice Emergy Lumumba was a fiery, erratic orator, a 35-year-old inexperienced politician with a driving, ruthless ambition. His lust for power and his ability to whip up an emotional crowd made him a force to be reckoned with in 1960 when the colonial rulers of the vast tract of the Belgian Congo felt the wind of change sweeping through Africa.

Foreseeing the explosive force of rising African nationalism, the Belgians had no great wish to pay the heavy price for hanging on to their African colony. But neither could they see any prospect for a smooth transition to independence as they began to hand over power to the people of the Congo in the elections of 1960. They were dismayed by the growing support for rebel leader Moise Tshombe who was leading the movement to wrench his own rich Katanga Province from the new independent Congo into a separate nation. But they watched most closely two political rivals who both swore to force Katanga to stay within the new Congo and who would hold the balance of power between them.

The Belgians were quietly satisfied when the election returned the quiet, educated civil servant Joseph Kasavubu to the post of President. They saw danger signs in the wave of popular support which swept Patrice Lumumba, a rebellious postmaster, into power as Prime Minister. Lumumba, they knew, had courted the promise of military backing from the Soviet Union to help him win office.

The new Prime Minister, expelled from a Roman Catholic mission school as a teenager for sexual promiscuity and later jailed for two years for embezzlement, confirmed their worst fears. Within weeks the enthusiastic and naive Lumumba found he had unleashed forces he could not control. The political theorists and policy managers of Moscow supervized his every move as the Congolese began to feel they were being freed from one foreign colonial ruler just in time to inherit another. Lumumba's reaction was to begin a bloody purge against dissident tribesmen using the resources of the teams of Russian technicians and military advisers pouring into the country.

Lumumba personally directed his troops to carry out the massacre of 3,000 Baluba tribesmen, flying his army to the scene in 19 Ilyushin jet transports provided by the Russians.

Some international observers condoned his ruthlessness as the brute force needed to weld the newly born country together. Others saw him provoking an increasingly bitter civil war.

Under pressure from the Belgians, President Kasavubu had Lumumba arrested and removed from office. There followed a cat and mouse game in which Lumumba escaped from house arrest and, according to his supporters, was greeted by cheering crowds in every village he visited.

The departing Belgians, who wanted to have a stable ally in the new Congo Republic to protect their commercial interests, were angered by Lumumba's freedom, although they seemed to regard him more as a nuisance than a serious menace, a naive troublemaker who would soon outlive his usefulness to his political controllers.

Lumumba was re-arrested in January 1961 and sent to an area where he could not expect any cheering crowds of villagers, the rebellious province of Katanga. Within a week he was dead, together with his two trusted followers Joseph Okito and Mauruce Mpolo.

But that was not the way the story was told ... Initially, Patrice Lumumba was reported to have escaped from custody yet again. A poker-faced Katanga Minister of the Interior Paul Munungo held a brief press conference to show newsmen the hole in the wall where he claimed Lumumba and his accomplices had tunnelled their way to freedom from their villa in Elisabethville, under the noses of their guards. 'We are offering a reward for their capture,' he explained.

His next press conference, three days later, was equally brief and subdued. Lumumba, according to the minister, had escaped from Elisabethville by car, travelling more than 321 km (200 miles) through unfriendly country, and stopped at a remote settlement in the bush outside the town of Kolwezi. There the villagers, anxious to claim the £3,000 reward, had promptly hacked him and his companions to death. A Katangese official had visited the site and confirmed the three men were buried in an unmarked grave.

All pressure from the journalists for further details was brushed aside.

'We forgot to specify on the reward posters that we wanted Lumumba captured alive', the Minister apologized. 'So the villagers are not to blame for his death. Besides he was a criminal so there's no harm done.'

And the location of the un-named village? It had to be kept secret, was the reply, to prevent any potentially ill-advized pilgrimages by Lumumba supporters. Lumumba's untimely death was doubtless a relief to the harassed Belgians. But the Russians who had been seen to be powerless to protect their protégé, were furious.

'Assassination' they cried and grandly set about planning a university for African revolutionaries in Moscow, to be named as a memorial to Patrice Lumumba. In the meantime they demanded the resignation of the Secretary General of the United Nations, the international body which was overseeing the Congo's transition to independence.

The wreckage of Dag Hammerskjoeld's aircraft

Being the target of scathing abuse and demands that he quit his job were nothing new for Dag Hammarskjoeld. The Scandinavian elder statesman suffered the violent criticism of Western leaders who claimed he was not making enough use of the multinational UN armed forces at his command to speed up the creation of the new Congo state. Eastern leaders complained bitterly that he interfered too much.

When Gurkha troops provided by India for the UN peace-keeping operation beat and killed hundreds of Katangan rebels, Hammarskjoeld shouldered the responsibility, burdened by the sharp condemnation of world leaders who were appalled by his mishandling of the delicate situation. Russian premier Nikita Krushchev branded the UN official: 'A bloody handed lackey of the colonial powers'.

Hammarskjoeld simply went about his job as he saw it, impartially trying to be a peaceful midwife in the bloody and painful birth of the new Congo.

He seems not to have hesitated when he received the invitation from the Katangan rebel leader, Moise Tshombe, to meet him for talks on a possible peace initiative in the battle between the breakaway province and the rest of the Congo. The talks were to be held in neutral territory, in Ndola in Rhodesia, the neighbouring country to Katanga.

From the outset, the flight was surrounded in furtive secrecy and disastrous planning. Hammarskjoeld planned to fly from Leopoldville in a DC4 Skymaster plane, specially prepared at the airport for him. At the last minute, to avoid the waiting packs of journalists, he switched to another aircraft, a DC6 airliner.

The DC6 was certainly better equipped. It was the personal plane of General Sean McKeown, commander of the UN forces in the Congo. With its four powerful engines it had a comfortable cruising range of more than 4,000 km (2,500 miles).

But 24 hours before, the DC6 had come under attack as Congolese soldiers had blasted one of its engines with anti-aircraft fire. The DC6 had been hastily repaired and left unguarded in a dispersal bay at Leopoldville Airport.

The pilot, Per-Erik Hallonquist, added to the confusion, designed to throw journalists off the track, by filing a flight plan for a journey to a small airport in Kisai Province, about halfway along his secret route to the Rhodesian border town of Ndola.

He took off in mid-afternoon, with 15 other people on board, including a radio operator with no flying experience. Only minutes before becoming airborne did he realize that the page of maps and instructions giving details of his approach to Ndola, was missing from his flight briefing book.

The flight, however, seems to have begun uneventfully. After four hours flying, around his expected time of arrival, Hallonquist contacted Ndola air traffic control, asking about weather and runway conditions and reporting his intention to descend from high altitude to 9,700 km (6,000 ft), obviously preparing to begin his approach to the airport.

The control tower responded and waited. And waited and waited ...

Two and a half hours later, the controllers were startled to see the DC6 approach the airfield from the south-west, flying from deep inside Rhodesian territory as if it had overshot its destination by 160 km (100 miles) and was re-tracing its route. There had been consternation over the non-arrival of the DC6 but no panic. The aircraft still had enough fuel to stay aloft for another seven hours.

Hallonquist radioed again, with matter-of-fact calmness. 'I have your runway lights in sight ... Overhead Ndola ... Now descending.' Without the benefit of radar coverage, the air traffic control staff peered into the night, beyond the runway, waiting for a glimpse of the DC6. They saw only a sudden brilliant flash of flame. Then darkness. The DC6, turning on its final approach, had struck a tree with its wingtip and plunged burning into a forest close to the airport.

In the confusion, darkness and thick jungle, it took almost two hours for the first rescue team to locate the aircraft. They found bodies scattered all round the strewn wreckage. And they found the macabre clues which seemed to show that the final fatal plunge of the DC6 might not have been a simple misjudgement by its pilot.

The fuselage, near the flight deck, was peppered with bullet holes. The body of Dag Hammarskjoeld lay sprawled in the aisle between the twisted seats. A few feet away was a revolver. And tucked into the lapel of his jacket was a playing card, the Ace of Spades.

Only one man was found alive that night, security officer Harry Jullian, an American. He was unconscious, suffering broken limbs and burns to 50 per cent of his body.

The next day the investigators began to piece together the evidence. Hammarskjoeld had not died instantly of his injuries and he had not been shot. But the long delay in reaching the crash site meant that he died without being able to tell anything about the final few minutes of the flight.

Smashed bottles of whisky and brandy had been found in the wreckage, adding weight to reports that many of the flight crew and and security escort had boarded the plane weary and staggering after an all-night binge in a Leopoldville drinking club.

Technical experts found that the plane's altimeter had an inexplicable mechanical error of 37 m (1,200 ft), giving the pilot a deceptively safe reading of his height above the ground.

And one witness had reported hearing the whistle of jets above the airport only minutes before the DC6 crashed. The only jets within flying distance were the fighter aircraft of the rebel Katangese, 160 km (100 miles) away in Elisabethville.

Later that day Sergeant Jullian recovered consciousness. The investigators sat by his bedside.

'Where had you been during the missing two hours?' they asked. 'Why didn't you arrive when you were expected?''

'Mr Hammarskjoeld told us to turn back, he didn't say why,' was all the injured man could reply. He died two days later without speaking again.

A Rhodesian inquiry firmly blamed the crash on pilot error. Later a five-man UN Commission sifted through the evidence, considering sabotage and gunfire, and concluded that the cause of the crash still remained unexplained.

The Katangese, who had bitter memories of their treatment at the hands of the UN's Gurkha troops, refused to take part in any investigation.

If Dag Hammarskjoeld's plane was brought down by a time delay bomb or a gunfight in the cabin or an attack by jet fighters, no one gloated openly or took the blame for killing him.

But who put the mark of death, the Ace of Spades, across the chest of the dying statesman? Could it have been someone who shared that last flight with him?

Streets of Fear

He struck terror into the heart of London's East End. Fear and panic stalked the streets, and the mention of his name would silence a noisy pub.

Jack the Ripper was what they called him ... this twisted and mysterious killer who preyed on women forced by poverty to sell their bodies for a few pennies in the alleys and backstreets.

Jack the Ripper's reign of terror was mercifully short. Three months after he first struck, on a warm summer night a century ago, he claimed his last victim.

He is known to have murdered at least five women, and some criminologists believe the true tally is eleven. But his identity has remained a mystery. Scotland Yard files on the case will be made public in 1992 but they are expected to cast little new light on the mysterious attacker.

One of Jack the Ripper's victims was found behind this shop

All that is known for certain is that the Ripper had some medical knowledge and was left-handed – as police surgeons examining the remains of his victims noticed. He is believed to have been a tall, slim, pale man with a black moustache. Several people, including a policeman, saw such a man hurrying away from the vicinity of the crimes. In each case he was said to be wearing a cap and a long coat, and to walk with the vigorous stride of a young man.

The terror began shortly after 05.00 on the morning of 7 August 1888, when a man found the mutilated body of a woman on the landing of a Whitechapel tenement block.

She was identified as Martha Turner, a prostitute. She had been stabbed several times.

The murder of East End prostitutes was no rare thing in those days. London's docks were always filled with ships from around the world, and foreign seamen packed the pubs and sleazy drinking dens near the waterfront.

But the mutilation was unusual. And when a second, similar murder happened 24 days later, fear brought a chill to the warm late summer evenings.

The body of 42-year-old Mary Ann Nicholls – known as Pretty Polly – was found in the early hours of 31 August. Mary had been trying to earn fourpence, the price of a dosshouse bed, with perhaps a few coppers more for a couple of tots of gin. When last seen she was approached by a tall, pale man, and disappeared into the shadows with him. She was found with her throat cut, and her body savagely mutilated.

A detective said, 'Only a madman could have done this.' And a police surgeon added: 'I have never seen so horrible a case.'

A week later the Ripper struck again, killing 'Dark Annie' Chapman, who was 47 and dying of tuberculosis. Her disembowelled body was found by a porter from Spitalfields market, her few possessions neatly laid out alongside.

On 25 September, 18 days after Annie's death, a letter arrived at the Central News Agency in Fleet Street. It read:

'Dear Boss, I keep on hearing that the police have caught me. But they won't fix me yet ... I am down on certain types of woman and I won't stop ripping them until I get buckled.

Grand job, that last job was. I gave the lady no time to squeal. I love my work and want to start again. You will soon hear from me, with my funny little game.

I saved some of the proper red stuff in a ginger beer bottle after my last job to write with, but it went thick like glue and I can't use it. Red ink is fit enough, I hope. Ha, ha!

Next time I shall clip the ears off and send them to the police just for jolly.'

The letter was signed 'Jack the Ripper'. It was the first time the name had ever been used. And it immortalized this twisted and mysterious killer of the London backstreets.

The next victim was Elizabeth 'Long Liz' Stride, whose body was found behind a factory gate by a policeman on the morning of Sunday 30 September. She had not been mutilated, and police suspected the Ripper had been disturbed in his grisly task.

But he soon found another victim, and left the only clear clue to his identity. The bloody remains of 40-year-old Catherine Eddowes were found about 1.5 km from where Liz's body had been discovered. She was the most terribly mutilated victim so far. Her ears had been cut off. And a trail of blood from the corpse led to a chalked message on a wall: 'The Jewes are not men to be blamed for nothing.'

But this one clue was not examined properly. Sir Charles Warren, head of the Metropolitan Police, fearing it might provoke an outbreak of violent anti-semitism, had it erased and kept secret.

Rumours swept through the streets.

Some said the Ripper carried his instruments of death in a little black bag, and any innocent passer-by carrying such a bag risked being set upon by fear-crazed locals.

He was a foreign seaman ... a Jewish butcher ... a mad doctor ... a Russian sent by the Czar to try to cause unrest in London ... a puritan intent on ridding the streets of vice ... a mad midwife who hated prostitutes.

Some said the Ripper must be a policeman, which was why he could prowl the streets at night without arousing suspicion. An even wilder theory held that he was Queen Victoria's eldest grandson, Prince Albert Victor, the Duke of Clarence.

The Ripper claimed his last victim, Mary Kelly, a 25-year-old blonde, on 9 November. Unlike the others she was young and attractive. One of the last people to see her alive was a George Hutchinson, when she approached him and asked him for money to pay her rent. He said he could not help, and noticed her approach a slim, well-dressed man with a trim moustache and a deerstalker hat.

When rent collector Henry Bowers called on Mary next morning he could get no reply. Seeing the window to her room open, he reached in and pushed aside the sacking curtain. He took one horrified look at the sickening sight inside and ran for the landlord. He said later: 'I shall be haunted by it for the rest of my life.'

With Mary's death, the Ripper's reign of horrific crimes ended as suddenly as it had begun.

Two convicted murderers claimed to be the Ripper. One, who poisoned his mistress, said when arrested: 'You've got Jack the Ripper at last.' But there was no evidence to support his claim.

Another killer, sentenced to death, cried out as the gallows trapdoor opened: 'I am Jack the ...' But he had been in America when the Ripper's murders were committed.

Some policemen believed they knew the Ripper's identity. The Assistant Commissioner of the Metropolitan Police said in 1908: 'In saying that he was a Polish Jew I am merely stating a definitely established fact.'

Inspector Robert Sagar, who had been on the case and died in 1924, wrote

A *Punch* satire on the police's inability to catch the murderer

in his memoirs: 'We had good reason to suspect a man who lived in Butcher's Row, Aldgate. We watched him carefully. There was no doubt that this man was insane and, after a time, his friends thought it advisable to have him moved to a private asylum. After he was removed, there were no more Ripper atrocities.'

Author and broadcaster Daniel Farson, who for several years ran a riverside East End pub, has offered another solution. He said recently that he suspects Montagu John Druitt, a failed barrister with medical connections and family history of mental instability.

Farson based his belief on the notes of Sir Melville Macnaghten, who became head of the CID in 1903. Mcnaghten named three main suspects – a Polish tradesman, probably Jewish, who hated women, a Russian doctor and Druitt.

A few weeks after the death of Mary Kelly, Druitt's body was found floating in the Thames.

After that Jack the Ripper claimed no more victims. But there is a postscript to the affair . . .

Two victims of Jack the Ripper have returned to haunt the scenes of his heinous crimes, according to witnesses. The ghost of Mary Ann Nicholls, the 42-year-old prostitute who was the second of the grisly butcher's six victims, has been seen dozens of times – glowing mysteriously in the gutters of Durward Street, Whitechapel, close to where the Ripper left her lying after cutting her throat and stomach. Piercing screams heard nearby, in Hansbury Street, Spitalfields, are said to be those of another of his victims – 47-year-old Annie Chapman.

Jack the Stripper

A mass murderer called Jack the Stripper roamed the streets of west London for 12 savage months. The killer, like the Ripper before him, preyed on prostitutes. And like the Ripper, he was never caught.

He left his victims naked, with one or more of their front teeth removed. And perhaps, if one or two of their men customers had come forward, some of them would still be alive today.

The Stripper's reign of terror began when the body of pretty, 30-year-old

Hannah Tailford was found on the Thames foreshore near Hammersmith Bridge, in west London, on 2 February 1964. All her clothes were missing except her stockings, which were rolled down to her ankles, and her pants, which had been stuffed in her mouth probably to stifle her screams.

Hannah, small and slim, had come to London from Heddon-on-the-Wall, Northumberland. She had a wild background and specialized in group sex sessions. Police found cameras and lighting equipment at her flat, and she had apparently taken compromising photographs at her orgies.

There was a theory that she might have been killed by someone she was blackmailing.

Enquiries revealed only that she had last been seen nine days before her death. And the pathologist reported that she had been pregnant.

The Stripper's second victim, 25-year-old Irene Lockwood, was discovered on 8 April on the Thames foreshore at Duke's Meadow, Chiswick, about 274 m (300 yd) upstream from where Hannah's body had been found.

Again, police at first suspected blackmail as a motive. Then a man stepped forward and confessed he was the killer. He was able to describe Irene accurately, and he was charged.

But Jack the Stripper struck again during the trial. The man was acquitted and returned to obscurity.

The third victim, 22-year-old Helen Barthelemy, was a petite Scots girl who had worked as a circus trapeze artist and as a stripper on Blackpool's Golden Mile. Her body was found on 24 March, at Brentford, and gave police some useful leads.

Unlike the others, the body was found on dry land, in an alley. Her clothes had clearly been removed after death. Four of her front teeth were missing, and traces of spray paint were found on her body.

Police began a systematic examination of workshops and garages in the area where spray paint was used, and appealed to the public for help. The publicity seemed to scare off the killer. There were no more killings for three months.

The Stripper's fourth victim, 30-year-old Mary Fleming, was found on 14 July, propped up against the garage door of a private house in Chiswick. She too, was naked, and her body also showed small traces of spray paint.

The discovery was made at 05.00 by a chauffeur who lived directly opposite. Painters working overnight at business premises nearby reported hearing the doors of a vehicle being slammed as it reversed. A few minutes later it drove off at speed but the men could not read the number plate because they were behind frosted glass.

Scotland Yard scientists established that the paint found on the victims was of a type and colour range in use by some car manufacturers. It seemed fairly certain that the bodies had been kept in or near premises used for car body repairs.

By now terror was stalking the streets of west London. Most women refused to go out alone after dark, and the area's prostitutes walked the streets in twos and threes.

The fifth victim was discovered under a pile of rubbish in a car park at Hornton Street, Kensington, on 25 November. She had last been seen alive on 23 October, and had been dead for about a month. The girl, 20-year-old Glasgow-born Margaret McGowan, had been involved in the Profumo scandal of the previous year, and had given evidence at the trial of Stephen Ward. Using the name Frances Brown, she had told how Ward had sketched her at his flat.

Everyone connected with the Profumo scandal was traced and questioned, and all were eliminated.

Margaret had been with another prostitute, Kim Taylor, for 24 hours before she disappeared. She had drunk about 19 whiskies before the two of them went out soliciting together in Portobello Road.

They were picked up by two men in separate cars, and it was arranged that all four should meet at Chiswick Green. But Kim and her customer lost the other car in Bayswater Road, and Margaret was not seen alive again.

It was nearly a year after Hannah Tailford, the Stripper's first victim, disappeared, that he claimed his last.

She was 28-year-old Bridget 'Bridie' O'Hara, who vanished from her home and usual haunts on 11 January 1965. That evening she visited the Shepherd's Bush Hotel, a pub, and was recognized by several male acquaintances, who spoke to her. The pub closed at 23.00 and she probably died soon after that.

Her body was found on 16 February behind a small workshop alongside a busy railway line. She had been strangled and the body had clearly been stored somewhere and dumped shortly before its discovery.

As with the other victims, there were traces of paint, plus specks of oil, suggesting she had been kept near some kind of machinery.

Chief Superintendent John du Rose, who was leading the murder hunt, marked off a wide sector of west London and sent out hundreds of detectives to visit every possible garage, workshop and factory that might have held the body. Police began taking the numbers of kerb-crawling cars, and the drivers were brought in for questioning.

As a psychological ploy, du Rose increased the publicity being given to the case, and dropped hints that he was getting close to being able to identify the Stripper.

Police discovered a building housing a transformer where the bodies of

Helen and Bridie had been stored. It was close to a paint-spray shop, at the rear of a factory on the Heron Trading Estate in Acton.

Now du Rose concentrated his hunt on the immediate area. But still the killer eluded the teams of detectives. At first they thought they had scared him off. But soon it became clear that the killings had stopped altogether.

On a hunch, du Rose began a search through all the suicides, accidental deaths and jailings in London since Bridie's murder. He came up with a prime suspect – a 45-year-old man who had lived in south London and had worked for a security firm in west London. He had a van and the paint-spray shop was one of the buildings he patrolled. Shortly after the discovery of Bridie's body he had committed suicide, leaving a note saying he was 'unable to stand the strain any longer'.

To save the feelings of his wife and children, who were quite baffled by his death, police did not name the man.

Was he really Jack the Stripper? Probably no one will ever know.

Death in the Churchyard

Nurse Olive Bennett was leading a double life ... and it was to bring her a violent death. For most of her adult life, 45-year-old Olive had lived in the prim, starchy style expected of a midwife and spinster. But since joining the staff of a maternity home at Tiddington, Warwickshire, she had begun to kick over the traces.

She had taken up smoking, and was making large withdrawals from her Post Office savings account. On her evenings off she would spend an hour or two dressing and making-up, and usually take the bus to nearby Stratford-on-Avon.

She became a familiar figure in the town's old-world pubs, chain-smoking and drinking large sherries. She would often arrive back at the nurses' home by taxi in the early hours of the morning. Once she told a colleague she had been with her boyfriend.

So nothing seemed amiss when she was still not back by midnight on 23 April 1954.

It was Shakespeare's 390th birthday, and all Stratford was celebrating. The Memorial Theatre was staging *A Midsummer Night's Dream* and restaurants and pubs were packed.

That night Olive caught the 20.15 bus to Stratford. Her first call was probably the Red Horse Hotel, where she was seen drinking until 21.00. She was seen later in other pubs. In one she said to a man: 'I've had five schooners of sherry already. Aren't I a naughty girl?' The night porter at the Red Horse Hotel recalled seeing her again at 23.45 standing outside the hotel. He was the last man to see Olive alive.

Next morning the gardener at Holy Trinity Church beside the river noticed a headstone was missing. Nearby were a pair of spectacles a woman's brown shoe and a set of lower dentures.

Within hours police had found Olive's body in the river, weighted down with the missing headstone. She had been strangled.

Her diary contained the names of several men friends. All were questioned and eliminated from police enquiries. Every soldier at the nearby Long Marston camp was interviewed.

Scotland Yard was called in, and the legendary Detective Superintendent Jack Capstick – famed for his motto 'Softly, softly, catchee monkey' – arrived to head the case. Hundreds more people were questioned, but still the police drew a blank. Reluctantly, Capstick returned to the Yard leaving the case wide open.

Not until eight years later did two sisters come forward with a story that could be linked with the murder. The girls, both bus conductresses, from Leamington Spa, said they had been in Stratford on the night of the murder and had been picked up by two soldiers. At 23.00 the four of them had gone for a walk in Holy Trinity churchyard.

The older girl said: 'We were standing by some graves when my soldier began getting fresh. I told him to stop it.' The soldier said, apparently as a joke, that he would push her in the river, with a headstone to weigh her down.

The girls had kept quiet at the time because one was married, and the other did not want her mother to know. Perhaps if they had spoken up at the time Olive's murderer would have been found and brought to justice. The time lapse made that impossible.

Painstakingly the police traced and re-interviewed soldiers who had been at Long Marston camp at the time of the murder. Again, they drew a blank, and today it seems unlikely that the mystery of **who** killed Olive Bennett will ever be solved.

The Arm in the Shark Case

The story hit the headlines on Anzac Day – 25 April 1935. It was labelled in shrieking type across the front pages as 'The Arm In The Shark Case'. To incredulous newspaper readers that day, to police and forensic experts, it was one of the most bizarre mysteries ever.

The mystery began in the Sydney seaside suburb of Coogee. Fisherman Bert Hodson had set out in his small boat to examine lines he had baited with mackerel about 1.5 km off shore. He was after shark. Hodson was in luck: he found not one but two of the dread killers. One small shark was already firmly hooked to one of his lines. Another, a 4.2 m (14 ft) tiger shark, was in the process of devouring the smaller one. The fisherman hauled in the line and found the tiger shark was now firmly ensnared. Turning his boat for the shore, he headed home with the creature in tow.

Hodson would normally have killed the shark and hung it on the boathouse scales. But the fisherman's brother, Charles, ran an aquarium at Coogee and Bert knew that the prize tiger shark would provide an excellent attraction for the paying customers who crowded down from the city.

And so it proved. The shark circled menacingly round the aquarium to the delight of the trippers for a few days. Then, on 25 April the fascination on the faces of the visitors turned to horror as they witnessed the most astonishing spectacle. The tiger shark went into convulsions. It surged around the water, disgorging the contents of its stomach: rats, birds, parts of the smaller shark – and a human arm.

Charles Hodson acted swiftly. He fished out the arm and telephoned the police. They found the grisly specimen to be the left arm of a man, with a tattoo of two boxers slugging it out. Attached was a length of rope.

At first, police put the case down as a shark attack on a lone swimmer or yachtsman until, over the days, their suspicions became aroused. No one had been reported missing off a Sydney beach. And a police surgeon who examined the arm claimed that it had not be bitten off by a shark but cleanly amputated with a sharp knife.

Fingerprints were taken of the hand and, although they were blurred, experts were able to match the prints of the thumb and ring finger with those of a man in police files. They belonged to James Smith, who ran a billiard room grandly titled the Rozelle Sports Club, and who had once been arrested for illegal bookmaking. Smith had been missing from his home for 28 days. His brother, Edward, positively identified the arm but was unable to give any hint as to Smith's movements. And all that the victim's wife, Gladys, knew was that her husband had left home saying that he was taking a party on a paid fishing trip.

The police sought out Smith's friends. One of them John Brady, was not easy to find for he was wanted by Tasmanian police on a forgery charge. But he was eventually run to ground on 17 May, living with his wife in a small flat in north Sydney. Under interrogation, Brady admitted having stayed with Smith in a cottage at Cronulla, on the same stretch of coastline as the shark had been caught, but denied knowing anything about the crime.

Over the next few months, divers and chartered aircraft searched the waters of Cunnamatta Bay, near Cronulla, hoping to find further clues.

The police had a theory, however. They believed that Smith went to stay with Brady at Cronulla to plan their next fraud, but that the two men fell out over the sharing of the loot. Brady, they believed, killed his accomplice and hacked up the body. He placed the remains in a metal trunk – but could not fit in the arm. So he roped it to the outside of the trunk and dumped the terrible evidence into the sea. A small shark, attracted by the blood, attacked the trunk, severing the rope with its razor-sharp teeth. As the arm floated free, the shark swallowed it whole.

The shark's next meal was the mackerel on Bert Hodson's line. And that was when the shark became a meal for the larger tiger shark.

The police theory sounded far-fetched. But the 'Arm In The Shark Case' was soon to prove that fact can be even stranger than fiction.

The crime that detectives believed Smith and Brady had been plotting was an insurance fraud over a yacht that had apparently disappeared. Police interviewed the yacht's former owner, whom they regarded as a key witness. But the day before an inquest was due to be held into Smith's death, the witness was found shot dead in his car beneath the approaches to Sydney's famous Harbour Bridge.

The following day, detectives received another blow. The coroner who was to have held the inquest ruled that he could not do so without a complete body. Nevertheless, Brady was charged with murder and sent for trial.

The trial lasted only two days. The judge refused to admit as evidence signed statements that had been taken from the witness before he was found shot dead. Without this evidence, the jury was directed to acquit Brady. Two men were charged with murdering the witness, but they too were acquitted.

Brady continued his career of crime. In all, he spent more than 20 years of his life in jail. During all that time, the only person who knew the full facts of the 'Arm In The Shark Case' never once hinted at what the truth might be.

And the full story never will be known. John Brady suffered a heart attack at the age of 71 in a prison repatriation hostel. His secret died with him.

The Motorway Monster

The brutal killing of an attractive woman hitchhiker led to Britain's biggest-ever motorway murder hunt. In all, 1,500 police officers quizzed more than 125,000 people and took nearly 50,000 statements in their fruitless bid to track down the killer of schoolteacher Barbara Mayo.

Tall, dark-haired Barbara set off from her flat in Hammersmith, London, in October 1970 to hitchhike to Catterick, Yorkshire, to pick up her boyfriend's car which had broken down there. Her own car had been giving her trouble and she did not want to risk a breakdown in it. Two days after she had left London, her boyfriend physics graduate David Pollard, reported her missing.

Four days later a miner rambling with his family in a wood just off the M1 at Ault Hucknall, near Chesterfield, Derbyshire, stumbled on her partly clothed body under a pile of leaves. Barbara, aged 24, had been raped and strangled.

Police knew it would be a tough case to crack. For the most baffling murder cases are those in which an element of association between victim and killer is missing. In the case of Barbara Mayo, there were no locals with helpful information; she was found 321 km (200 miles) from home and there was nothing to connect her murderer with her or the area where she was found. The killer could have been a commercial traveller, a commuter or a driver looking for casual sex with hitchhikers.

The police investigators – headed by Detective Chief Superintendent Charles Palmer of Scotland Yard – followed up every lead. They spent months checking thousands of Morris 1000 Travellers after a witness said he had seen Barbara, or a girl fitting her description, in a white Morris Traveller at Kimberley, Nottinghamshire. At that time more than 100,000 of this type of car were still on the road. Each owner had to be traced and eliminated.

The murder hunt also revealed something of the murky world of the motorway hitchhiker. In tests along the M1, police discovered that a man might have to wait between 30 minutes and two hours for a lift. But an attractive girl would be picked up in minutes. It seemed to indicate that there were men who drove on motorways simply to pick up girl hikers – and one of them might have picked up Barbara.

But the most worrying aspect was that girls, knowing the dangers they faced, still hitchhiked alone – often wearing provocative clothing to catch the eye of the drivers.

Police set up checkpoints along 320 km (200 miles) of the M1 between London and Leeds and asked motorists: 'Were you on this motorway 14 days ago? Did you see this girl?'

Each driver was shown a picture of Barbara with this description: 'Barbara Janet Mayo, aged 24 years, 1.7 m (5 ft 9 in), slim build, high cheekbones, brown eyes, light tanned complexion, good teeth ... wearing navy-blue coat with eight silver buttons, gold and tan brocade slacks, hipster style, lilac jersey, blue socks, corduroy lace-up shoes.' But nothing led the police any closer to 'The Monster of the Motorway', as the newspapers dubbed the ruthless killer.

Next, police plastered posters with Barbara's picture and a detailed description all over Britain. Chief Superintendent Palmer said: 'I let it be known that if any motorist who had given a girl a lift on the M1 on 12 October came forward, I would meet him anywhere – and his wife would not be told.' But nobody came forward.

A London policewoman impersonating Barbara went from Barbara's flat by tube to Hendon, where the M1 then began. She stood at the roadside, thumbing lifts.

A butcher at Kimberley, Nottinghamshire, who saw the reconstruction on television told police: 'I'm sure she came into my shop and asked for two freshly cooked faggots.' She had then crossed the road and walked down a hill towards the main road.

Was it Barbara Mayo? Or just another girl who looked like her? The question remains unanswered.

Charles Palmer said:

'I still hope that somebody, somewhere will come forward with vital information. And though there are people who can live with murder on their conscience, I still don't rule out the possibility that the person or persons responsible for Barbara's death will confess.'

There is one person, however, who believed that the police were largely wasting their time in the nationwide hunt for Barbara's killer. That person is her mother, widow Mrs Marjorie Mayo. She said:

'I have never believed Barbara was hitchhiking. I believe her murder took place in London and was carried out by somebody in a bad crowd Barbara had got in with. Her body was probably taken in her own car and left by the M1 to put the police off the trail. She came to see me the day before she disappeared. She said: 'Mummy I'm so frightened.' But before she could explain, some people called at the house and the conversation was lost.

Barbara is never far from my thoughts – she is still very real to me. And I don't believe her murder will ever be solved.'

Death of the Black Dahlia

The corpse found on an undeveloped building site in a Los Angeles suburb on 15 January 1947 had been savagely mutilated. It was the body of a young woman, cut in half at the waist and with the initials 'B. D.' carved into her thigh.

It was the use of those initials that gave the case its notoriety. They stood for 'Black Dahlia', the nickname given to a pretty 22-year-old small-time movie actress, Elizabeth Short. She was known simply as Betty or Beth to her friends. But she also revelled in the nickname of Black Dahlia because of her liking for jet-black clothes. And, from fingerprints, the body was identified as being hers.

Elizabeth Short's brief life was not a happy one. She had been a juvenile delinquent but found love and a chance of a fresh start when she met a young serviceman. He proposed, they became engaged, then parted when he was posted overseas in World War 2.

He never came home – and his death sent Elizabeth on a downhill path. She turned to drink and tried her luck as a bit-part actress in Hollywood. But jobs were hard to come by and she began working as a waitress by day and haunting sleazy bars and pick-up joints by night. The inevitable happened. Elizabeth started to accept money for her favours. She soon became known for her black apparel – including her black silk underwear.

The Black Dahlia had one further chance of rescue when a second lover proposed to her. Cruelly, he too died ... and Elizabeth's fate was sealed.

When the discovery of the poor girl's butchered body was reported in the Los Angeles newspapers, a strange reaction set in. Perhaps it was the photographs of the beautiful young victim – before and after death – that incited an astonishing spate of false reports and confessions.

The first came from a waitress who said she had heard two killers discussing the crime at a table. She gave the police a description – and inquiries revealed that the 'killers' were a couple of detectives having an off-duty coffee. Another tip came from a blonde dancer who told police: 'I'm meeting a man at First and Temple Streets at nine o'clock and I have reason to believe he's the Black Dahlia killer.' Detectives arrested the pair and took them in for questioning. The man turned out to be an innocent executive who had once spent a night with the blonde, following which she had been trying to blackmail him, without success. The 'tip off' to the police was just her way of applying extra pressure.

A photo of Elizabeth Short from her family album

One piece of evidence the police took much more seriously was a package sent to a Los Angeles newspaper enclosing a message cut from press headlines. It said: 'Here are Dahlia's belongings. Letter to follow.' The package also contained Elizabeth's social security card, her birth certificate and an address book – with one page torn out. Police said they believed that these articles had been removed from the body – no clothing was found at the scene – and that the missing page in the address book would have revealed the name of the killer. Fingerprints were taken from the social security card but they matched none in police files.

Later, a small-time underworld figure gave himself up to police, saying 'I killed the Black Dahlia.' This time detectives thought they had solved the case, because in Elizabeth's address book had been the name of a firm the suspect had once worked for. But a lie-detector test showed he was just another crank.

Years later, a 29-year-old army corporal was held on suspicion after volunteering the information: 'When I get drunk I get rough with women.' He knew many details of the killing. But again, he was finally dismissed as being mentally unbalanced.

In all, around 50 men have claimed they committed the murder – but the case of the Black Dahlia remains unsolved.

The Torso in the Trunk

Barely glancing up, the left-luggage clerk handed the man a ticket and heaved his heavy trunk into a corner of the office. 6 June, 1934 – Derby Day – was a busy day at Brighton railway station, with racegoers bound for Epsom and early holidaymakers swelling the usual commuting crowd.

The trunk was the seventieth to be deposited in a few hours and stuffing ticket CT1945 in his pocket, the man vanished in the crowd. He probably caught the next train to London.

It was not until 17 June that a clerk at Brighton station, noticing an unpleasant smell, opened the trunk and recoiled in horror at the terrible sight that met his eyes. Inside was the torso of a woman, wrapped in brown paper and tied around with a venetian blind cord.

An immediate search of other railway left-luggage offices led to the discovery of a suitcase containing the murder victim's severed legs at London's King's Cross station. It had been deposited there on 7 June.

What had happened to the head and arms? No one can be sure. But on 10 June a couple walking on the beach found a female human head in a pool.

Incredibly, they left it there and reported it to no one. When police heard of their find a month later and questioned them, they said they assumed someone had committed suicide by jumping off a cliff, and that the police had swept the remains they did not need into the sea.

Pathologist Sir Bernard Spilsbury said the murder had taken place on about 30 or 31 May, and that the victim had been a healthy young woman aged 21 to 28. She was about 1.7 m (5 ft 2 in) tall, weighed 54 kg (8 st 7 lb) and was pregnant. And there was no other means of identification.

Police came to the conclusion that the killer was probably a married man of some social standing who had an affair with the woman. She became pregnant, and when her condition became noticeable she asked him for help. He refused, and she threatened to tell his wife about their affair. They had a row, which became violent, and in the heat of the moment she was killed by a blow to the head.

On one of the pieces of brown paper detectives found the final part of a word written in blue pencil. The syllable FORD was easily recognizable, and the previous letter could have been a D or an L.

A woman working in a London warehouse came forward to identify the writing as her own. She regularly returned defective consignments to a confectionery firm at Bedford.

Police identified the brown paper she used as the type wrapped around the woman's remains. And they established that when such sheets arrived at the Bedford factory, they were re-used to dispatch goods to all parts of the country.

They followed every possible lead, but the trail went cold.

Chief Inspector Robert Donaldson from Scotland Yard took charge of the case. In an attempt to identify the victim, he launched a massive round-up of missing girls. In all, 732 who had left home were traced. He had detectives check every hospital, nursing home and doctor's surgery for details of women who had sought pre-natal advice. One London hospital alone produced 5,000 names.

Other detectives checked makers and retailers of trunks, and made discreet inquiries into thousands of purchases. But again they drew a blank.

Of all the thousands of clues that led nowhere, one statement seems to point to the killer. Porter Todd, at London Bridge Station, recalled helping a man with a heavy trunk on the 15.00 train for Brighton on 6 June. He had bought his cheap-day third-class ticket at Dartford, and was noticed by a girl on the same train. Only five cheap-day tickets to Brighton had been sold at Dartford that day. Four of the travellers were traced by the police ... but the fifth was never found.

Katyn – 1940

Murder is horrific enough when it involves just one victim, one body. But in the annals of unsolved crime there is one outrage against humanity so monstrous that it defies comprehension. It is the Katyn Massacre, one of the most cold-blooded atrocities in history, in which 4,300 innocent people were put to death. It is also a crime without a culprit – for no nation will accept responsibility for it.

The story begins on 17 September 1939, the day that Hitler and Stalin divided conquered and battle-ravaged Poland between them. From their sector, the Russians transported 15,000 Polish officers and intellectuals to labour camps in the Soviet Union.

About 500 were saved from the brutality of camp life to be indoctrinated into the communist system. The remainder languished in the camps until April 1940 – and then every one of them vanished.

In June 1941 the Nazis broke their peace pact with Stalin and marched into Russia. Two years later, German troops dug up an area of woodland at Katyn, near the Soviet city of Smolensk. They unearthed at least 4,300 bodies, which, from the documents still on the corpses, were proved to be those of some of the missing Poles.

The Nazis immediately blamed their communist foes for the massacre. But, in the midst of war, there was no way of proving the guilt of one nation or another.

Then, in 1944, the tide of war changed and the Russians recaptured Katyn from the retreating Germans. The Soviets immediately counter-claimed that it was the Nazis, not them, who had been responsible for the massacre.

The balance of the evidence, however, weighs against the Russians. It is reported that Soviet soldiers were sent to Katyn in 1940 and ordered to dig a pit 30.5 m (100 ft) long and 15 m (50 ft) wide. A cattle train then arrived with a human cargo. About 4,300 Poles were ordered out and marched to the wooded site, out of the direct view of the villagers. The Poles were then lined up in rows. The Russians strode down the ranks, shooting each man in the back of the head and rolling the corpse into the pit. When ammunition seemed to be running low, some of the prisoners had sawdust stuffed into their mouths in order to suffocate them and were then buried alive beneath the next line of victims to be shot.

According to one report, some of the Soviet soldiers refused to carry out the executions. They committed suicide, throwing themselves into the pit. The soldiers who obeyed their orders were later dispersed to other units around Russia.

The Soviet Union has never faltered in its vehement denials that it bears any guilt for the massacre. But in recent years, the evidence of Poles who escaped Stalin's purge and fled to the West has been threaded together to provide apparent confirmation of the German story.

In London in 1976, a 6 m (20 ft) cenotaph was unveiled to the memory of the 14,500 missing Poles, including the 4,300 killed in Katyn. But the British government failed to send an official representative to the ceremony, adhering to the line that the story of a massacre had not been proven.

Polish ex-servicemen, wearing their cherished wartime uniforms and rows of medals, paraded their colours before the black stone cenotaph. They wept openly when the widow of one of the massacre victims drew aside the British and Polish flags which draped the memorial and revealed the simple inscription: 'Katyn 1940'.

Whether the Russians were responsible for the massacre or not remains in question. Also a mystery is what happened to the other 10,000 Poles who were transported to Russian labour camps? How many other Katyns are yet to be exposed?